MARRIAGE
in
TRANSITION

CREATING CONNECTION THROUGH
UNCONTROLLABLE CHANGE

SEAN AND LANETTE REED

CONTENTS

INTRODUCTION

"Marriage is a lot like a roller coaster. You have extreme highs, and you can have some pretty extreme lows, but the ride is worth it."

— TERESA COLLINS

AS NEWLYWEDS, WE WHOLEHEARTEDLY BELIEVED NOTHING could tear us apart. We were unsuspecting, naive, and in love. The happy-go-lucky, lusting after one another kind of couple. You know the type: the hand-holding, movie-going, date night having, and talking all night long couple. We said "I do" at the altar just four months out of high school. Three months later, we moved into our first apartment and had our first child. All of this took place within a year of graduating high school. We were *young and in love*. We got married and merged our bank accounts. Accounts that held the little pocket change we called "income" at the time. Now, if you're keeping count, that's seven major transitions within a few sentences. It all took place within a year! These are memorable events and significant accomplishments. So, everything should be good, right? Well, not quite.

We lacked parenting experience. Yet there we were trying to raise a child as if we knew what we were doing. We never had bills in our names before moving in together. No one, at that time, showed us how to manage a budget together. Still, we tried our best to make the most out of every dollar that came our way. I'm sure some of you relate to all, or at least one of these experiences. When you encounter a problem, a new adventure, or a bigger blessing than you've ever managed, you feel like a deer in headlights. Life was moving on and moving fast. I mean, transitions are some of life's greatest moments, yet they all came with their own twists and turns that we were not ready for at the time. It was as if each blessing we acquired carried a new set of pressure, and frankly, we weren't prepared. Month after month, it seemed like we were trying to keep up with each day's demands. But in the process, we were growing apart. Through overnight work schedules, traffic jams, adjusting to in-laws, a barrage of financial problems, baby doctor's appointments, constant personality clashes, and preparing for our second child...We weren't partners united. We were more like a house divided. With each transition, we had to shift our way of life just to maintain the home. We weren't focused on our marriage. It became all about the tasks, and we became roommates.

Those long intimate talks we had became short arguments fueled by the frustrations of unmet expectations. With the mounting bills came longer hours at work. That handsome baby boy brought diaper duties and late nights of, "It's your turn to rock him to sleep." We found ourselves longing for intimacy that we didn't seem to have time for, or maybe *we just didn't take the time for it.*

When I look back at my reactions, early on in our marriage transitions, I ultimately failed to display compassion. At times, I was flat out unkind to my wife. I was selfish and looking out for my own needs. And I, Lanette, struggled with communicating what was on my heart in fear of his reactions, so I kept them to myself, which didn't help me, and got us nowhere.

We didn't realize then that both of us were responding to life changes in immature ways. Often leading to conflicting methods of processing and solving our problems. There was a division in our home because we didn't prepare to face the changing times together. I can't recall us sitting down to manage our expectations of transitions or attitudes towards one another. This made us easy prey for problems to pull us apart. The truth is, though, that the initial impact of transitions isn't the primary concern. It's the residual trauma that clings to couples afterward. The baggage that we carry into the future keeps us weighed down by the past. Our goal is to help you overcome the trauma of painful experiences from your past so that you can plot the course forward in relational unity.

Dr. Lisa Marie Bobby, a couples' counselor, says, "Couples can protect their relationships by learning early on to expect transitions and adopt an attitude of compassion, kindness, and generosity." The sooner that you accept this truth, the faster you can adopt the right attitude about transitions. No matter what stage your marriage is in, learning how to resolve conflicts is a must.

So, what exactly is a marriage transition? Well, it comes in many forms and arrives in different packages. I want to define it as *a time when partners are united in the process of changing from one state to another.* As you can imagine, throughout life, we are continually changing from one condition of life to another. This definition reminds me of Protestant wedding vows. The vows were captured in *The Book of Common Prayer,* by Thomas Cranmer, which dates back to 1549. "I take thee, to be my wedded husband or wife, to have and to hold from this day forward, for better or worse, for richer or poorer, in sickness and in health, to love and to cherish." In other words, we promise to face the most significant challenges this world throws at us *together.* These vows embody a commitment to ride the ups and downs of life as a team. Now, I'm not saying that everyone has to use these vows, but I think it's important to note that as far back as ancient Medieval times, people were well aware of the continually changing conditions of life.

One of the most significant challenges in a relationship is the management of expectations. Without realizing it, we may have entered into this life-long journey with a hope of monotony. As if there would be no, "for better or worse" version of either you or your partner. There is an internal longing for your lover to treat you in the best way that drew you towards them. Yet, in reality, from the moment we say, "I do," whatever constant we crave from our partner is challenged with each changing condition of life. In each challenging circumstance or even in prosperous seasons of life, each spouse reacts uniquely. They'll also be impacted by their experiences, both emotionally and physically. Making navigating seasons of life together more complicated than we realize since each spouse has their unique, deep need for stability in their most volatile seasons. We long for togetherness when the triumphs or tragedies of life may tear us apart.

To draw closer through a crisis and get better at going through life together, we've got to adjust our expectations of marriage as a whole. Instead of seeing our marriage journey on a straight, flat, and relatively unchanging road, we must envision it to be more like a rollercoaster. It's a ride that requires you to place your hands and feet inside the vehicle, and strap in with your partner because you're definitely in for the ride of your lives! You'll have the thrill of building a home together. Or, you may experience the tightly wound corner of more bills, more work, and consequently less time together. Then you'll scale the unbelievable heights of having children and go headfirst towards the lowest of life's lows with gut-wrenching grief and loss.

As we look back over our 22 years of marriage, three adult children, and 17 years of leading families as pastors, we can say that we've seen and experienced our fair share of marriage transitions.

We firmly believe that our responses during times of change can make or break a relationship. Beneath the pressures of transitional events, an array of emotions emerge like joy, exhaustion, peace, hopefulness, anxiety, or even depression. We've experienced those emotions firsthand as we've faced so many challenges over the years such as significant sickness's, financial ups and downs, failed business ventures, buying and selling homes, moving across the country, losing close loved ones, and the worst of all: suffering the loss of a child during pregnancy. Yes, we definitely loved one another, but we needed *more* than that. We needed tools for preparation, for the planned or unplanned, good or bad that came our way.

We've seen families rejoice in childbirth and, within a few years, begin to fight one another over parenting disagreements. We've prayed with couples standing at the crossroads of staying or leaving the city they loved, their family, and friends to pursue greener pastures in another place. We've talked with families that were paralyzed in the aftermath of financial mistakes. Although we may not be able to predict every situation that lies ahead, we've discovered that we can fortify our families for the transitions yet to come.

If someone were to ask us now what we didn't do when we first began, the answer is simple. We didn't *expect* the transitions, and therefore we didn't *prepare* for them. It was as if we said, "I do" and then set sail to "destination happily married", without a compass or a clue of what was to come. We weren't in the habit of managing well the things we had control over, so when the things we couldn't control hit, we were left with double the devastation. What we needed over 24 years ago is something that we realize now.

We decided to write this book together as we understand couples may face the same experience, but both interpret and react to them uniquely. It was also important to us that you receive the raw, transparent truth about seasons of change from both our perspectives. As we share stories of struggles and successes, you'll be able to see all of the whirlwinds and wins that transitions have to offer. The pages that follow are written to help you steer your train towards generational legacy and satisfaction in marriage. You'll notice at the end of each chapter, there are a set of questions designed to help you discover answers unique to your situation. We believe the ability to effectively assess the past while processing the best routes to the future are key to relational success.

ADJUSTING TO CHANGE

1

Earthquakes and the Aftermath

"You may encounter many defeats, but you must not be defeated. In fact, it may be necessary to encounter the defeats, so you can know who you are, what you can rise from, how you can still come out of it."

— MAYA ANGELOU

"YOU WON'T BE ABLE TO CONCEIVE NATURALLY, AND YOU should consider alternative fertility options." Their physician delivered this prognosis just one week away from the day they would stand before their family and say, "I do." As you can imagine, this was heartbreaking news to this young and extremely family-oriented couple. These two lovebirds met while working together at Disney World Resorts. She'd just graduated, and he was still in his junior year of college. Their story was straight out of a love novel. Waking up every morning in anticipation to see one another at work. Weekends were filled with laughter, love, and Mickey Mouse. But over the next few years, life would throw successive, unexpected punches and test their partnership's fortitude.

They both lost promising jobs and struggled to find work for long stretches at a time. While fighting to regain footing on career paths, they fought to stay above water financially. In the midst of all of that, one day, the husband collapsed with shortness of breath. Upon arriving at the ER, they discovered heart complications that led to extended hospitalization. Not too long afterward, a dear family member passed away, and they struggled to grieve while battling these other issues simultaneously. Let's just say it got *real* for this young couple rather quickly.

Suddenly, a ray of hope filled their hearts. Despite the doctor's prognosis, she miraculously became pregnant. For a brief moment, they had something, or at least someone to celebrate, but with the blessing of the baby came a new gamut of concerns. Some of the joy was sapped away, knowing this was a high-risk pregnancy and the lingering uncertainty of their daughter not making it to full-term. It was almost too much to bear. Added to the array of emotions were concerns for additional expenses in a home already strapped for cash. As their world was shaken to the core by these crushing transitions, they said, "Bringing a baby into the world should have been one of the happiest seasons of our marriage. Instead, it became the scariest."

That's when their communication took a deep dive. The ability to think and share their thoughts and feelings became difficult. She faced prenatal depression and anxiety and was hesitant to share what she was going through with her husband and other people. Still, they persevered and tried to make things work.

As she prepared to become a new mom, absorbing all of the parenting tips, and baby products, an endless checklist overwhelmed her. On top of that, making room for a new life meant the end of her old one, and this was frightening. She said, "I felt like becoming a mom was my last major life accomplishment, and there was nothing else after that." The husband, on the other hand, was just happy to become a proud papa. Not wanting to be a killjoy, she would mask her feelings every time he brought up the baby and deferred the conversation to whatever else he wanted to discuss. At home, she began to keep to herself and often stayed up late with never-ending thoughts coming to mind. The husband sensed something was off but didn't quite know how to put his finger on it. He figured she was just overwhelmed. But seven months into the pregnancy, she wasn't able to keep it bottled up anymore.

Due to her body fighting the birth of her baby and a high-stress work environment, she encountered a lack of sleep, depression, and anxiety resulting in seven months of bed rest. Their breaking point was a dark moment where she drove to work, overwhelmed with all that was happening, and decided not to go in. Having aimlessly gone around the city, she ended up by a lake and was contemplating suicide.

It's no wonder they found themselves in our office, desperate for marriage advice, tips, tricks, anything that could salvage their relationship in the aftermath of successive transitions. As I'm sure you can imagine, the effects of their painful experiences were multifaceted. Their bouts with grief, career challenges, and financial difficulties took a toll on their souls. Looking through the lens of their lives, we learn a powerful lesson. Couples may experience the same circumstances, but how they process problems may differ vastly. As these reactions collide, the atmosphere is combustible. This is where marriage transitions may cause relational trauma. Trauma can be defined as any experience that's too overwhelming for the mind and body to process appropriately. Now maybe you're familiar with relational trauma and you're saying, "Trauma? We've never experienced something of that magnitude." But a traumatic event can be categorized in two ways.

"Big T" or "Little T" trauma[1]

"Big T" is when a person has survived an event like a major earthquake, physical or sexual abuse. "Little T" represents an event like the loss of someone close to you, the betrayal of a friend, or being insulted by your spouse. For our purposes, we're exclusively referring to the "Little T" form of trauma.

Trauma intensifies our sense of survival. If you've ever been in an accident, a painful experience, or witnessed a shocking image, you know what it's like. In a triggered state, the mind, emotions, and body go into fight or flight mode. Our protective mechanisms go on high alert to perceived threats. It's important to note that they may very well be "perceived" rather than actual danger. In relationships, this may manifest in self-isolation, verbal outbursts, to excessive behavior. It's when your whole self seeks protection and safety from a perceived threat. Imagine watching a horror film late at night. As you lay your head down to sleep, a sense of restlessness abides as you hear the reminiscent creepy sounds of demon footsteps in the halls. Of course, you know full well that the film is fake. And in reality, the house always makes noise, the actors with makeup and CGI did a great job, and you're as safe as can be. But the mind still sends signals of potential threats, and your body reacts with unrest.

Bouts of yelling at each other, undergoing chronic misfortunes, suffering personal failure, or even physical harm at the hand of a loved one, are the breeding ground of all types of trauma. In some cases, it's the result of an absence of loving care never given from your spouse when it should have been. Leaving a person longing for what never happened, a sense of knowing your spouse genuinely cares for you. And our protective behaviors become a habit, reshaping our mindset to an ongoing triggered state.

---

1. Cathy O'Neal, "5 Signs of Relational Trauma." (Charis Counseling Center, July 20, 2017). https://www.chariscounselingcenter.com/blog/5-signs-of-relational-trauma/.

As you can imagine, there's a broad range of transitions that we face as couples. While reacting to these moments of change, it may bring out the very best or, at times, the worst in us. This one thing is for sure, your spouse and those who live in your house will receive *who you are* as you react to life circumstances.

For example, let's say one spouse has unresolved grief from the loss of a loved one. If they struggle with processing the shock of their loss, the trauma they experience may cause them to retreat internally. Leaving their spouse feeling that they've been rejected or feel neglected as they've been shut out. It gives birth to a cycle of mirroring one another's emotional state of mind. Or as the saying goes, hurt people, hurt people.

We went through a four-year process of trying to find the common denominators of problems that became dysfunctional cycles in our home. We discovered that long after the traumatic moments transpired, we were still living out of the residual effects, like strings attached to the past, causing self-sabotaging behavior. Trauma changed us on a cellular level. It also changed the ways that we treated one another. How we interacted as a family, made decisions, or spent our money were present actions that were rooted in past traumatic experiences. Had we not pursued freedom from the cycles, we wouldn't have been aware of what was going on below the surface, nor how to change it. But what we have found to be true is that the impact of trauma left untreated compounds over time.

In many ways, the aftermath of transitions mirror that of an earthquake. On the surface level, the buildings shake, but deep down within the earth, things have fundamentally changed. Our life circumstances are the surface level. The ramifications of actions taken in response to shared conditions can boost your productivity as a team. Or it may lead to perpetual dysfunction in the family's future. Because the mind is malleable, your experiences have the power to define who you are and how you view one another.

Earthquakes happen when fault lines shift, sending seismic waves in every direction, causing the ground to vibrate. Buildings vibrate as a result of the ground shaking violently. Tremendous damage takes place if the building isn't constructed to handle the powerful vibrations. Usually, the severity of ground shaking increases the closer you are to the fault. The initial waves are sent through the earth at speeds of about 15,000 miles per hour. These cause even the most stable structures to vibrate. Then another series of waves follow the initial blow, causing the structures to sway from side to side.

When the Ground Falls Beneath Our Feet

Some earthquakes cause an effect known as liquefaction. It happens when the surface level is clay or sand. Shaken so intensely, it temporarily loses strength, and it acts as a fluid rather than as a solid. Seismic waves impact its structure and cause some of the empty spaces to implode. I won't bore you with all the scientific details of how this occurs, but water combined with the soil enables a solid structure to behave like a fluid rather than a solid for a short time. In general, newly formed layers with loose sediment, combined with high water content are more susceptible to liquefaction. You may be saying, "What does this have to do with my marriage?"

Well, one day, my family took a trip to the beach on the Atlantic shoreline. I dug my toes deep within the sand, just on the edge of the waves. But with each successive wave that crashed into the shore, I felt the sand shifting beneath my feet. After a while, the ground liquefied, and I had to readjust. At that moment, I recalled the words of Jesus regarding houses built on sand:

> *"If you work the words into your life, you are like a smart carpenter who dug deep and laid the foundation of his house on bedrock. When the river burst its banks and crashed against*

the house, nothing could shake it; it was built to last. But if you just use my words in Bible studies and don't work them into your life, you are like a dumb carpenter who built a house but skipped the foundation. When the swollen river came crashing in, it collapsed like a house of cards. It was a total loss" (Luke 6:48-49 MSG).

How many marriages are attempting to establish beautiful looking homes on the inevitability of shifting sands? The tide is coming, and the waves will crash, and eventually, the house will collapse. After 22 years of marriage, we can guarantee that the flood is coming, and every transition will test what you're made of. You both must learn and apply to your marriage the wisdom of God's Word. That is the solid rock that you build your family on, rather than shifting sands of man's opinion or societal trends.

The Aftershocks of Relational Trauma

What's terrifying about earthquakes is that aftershocks will likely follow up the initial blow. Aftershocks are earthquakes in their own right. Though their force is smaller than the first impact, they're no less dangerous. What's worse is that the radius of damage expands from the epicenter. They can last for weeks, months, or even years. The higher the initial earthquake, the more impactful the after-effects.

Christine McVie said, "I felt very at home in California, but the place is prone to earthquakes, and the one in 1994 scared the life out of me. For months afterwards, I felt that every time I sat down, I should have put on a seatbelt." Christine's example of her earthquake survival exposes the effects of post-traumatic stress. This occurs when triggers remain undiscovered or unresolved in our lives. We'll discuss this more throughout the book. But for now, the point we're emphasizing is that the initial disappointment, financial setback, breach of trust, or heated argument, runs deeper than what's seen above ground. Below the surface, fault lines are forming and possibly getting longer within the bedrock of the soul. And it doesn't just affect you, but your family as well.

The origin of earthquakes is fault lines. These are fractures within earth's crust. Sometimes these cracks are tiny. I'm talking hairline thin with barely detectable movement between the sliding plates. "Little T" trauma is similar to those hairline fractures when an insult is given to your spouse in an argument. You'd think people could get over it. But what if that insult is a trigger from a childhood experience? Those words said in the heat of the moment resurface something deep within their hearts. And it will leave you wondering, "What's the big deal? Why are they so sensitive?"

In other cases, those fault line fractures are more extensive because they're caused by something like a breach of trust. There are many different levels at which this can occur. For example, a wife catches her husband watching porn. Or, perhaps a husband finds out his wife's been flirting with an old fling on social media. Maybe the couple's world has been shaken to the core in the event of infidelity.

When couples face life challenges, they may rub each other the wrong way. When not addressed correctly, division seeps in, just like the separations within the earth. It leaves the opportunity for more earthquakes to come in the future. Now there are different types of fault lines, just as we have different lines of division within marriage.

Strike-slip Faults[2]

Strike-slip faults have rocks sliding *past* each other horizontally (like the San Andreas Fault Line). At some point, we've gone on

---

2. Becky Oskin, "Fault Lines: Facts About Cracks in the Earth," LiveScience (Purch, November 30, 2017). https://www.livescience.com/37052-types-of-faults.html.

strike. We've reached a relational impasse over differing opinions. It becomes a matter of who's right, versus who's wrong. It's the classic case of couples clashing over the best route to take for their future. When both spouses choose their own way, they slip into opposing directions. This kind of behavior will inevitably result in internal friction, and instead of steady growth, they become stagnant. It lays a foundation for a dysfunctional pattern that repeatedly plays out like this. They argue, more specifically, the same kind of disagreement they've had many times before, but with no resolution.

Regardless of the frustration they share over the fact that they've routinely faced similar clashes, they continue to try, yet again, to 'fix' their spouse. Expending emotional energy and wasted time that ends in insults against each other. The issues at hand remain unsolved. Now that they're both, "in their feelings," a numbness intensifies as well as personal pride. Troubleshooting the initial problem has triggered pain that leaves both people emotionally wounded. Eventually, someone storms out, and concedes for the sake of ending the misery of the moment. The air has gone out of the room for reaching any form of agreement as they both doggedly defend their own point of view. They've virtually gone on strike, a stalemate of sorts resulting from seemingly being unheard, wronged or misunderstood. This cycle can build up a toxic atmosphere of reoccurring feelings of rejection and hopelessness.

Normal Faults

Normal faults are where two blocks of crust begin to *pull apart*. This creates a relational valley like The Basin and Range Province in North America. These normal faults are spreading apart the earth's crust. What some couples may not realize is that their dysfunctional behaviors have become their "normal." As a result, their relationship is slowly but surely pulling apart. Over time their reoccurring faults have caused emotional distress, leading to distrust. So, though they're in the same home, they may be isolated. Living as a shell of themselves as a protective mechanism, while attempting to avoid confrontation.

Ultimately, they live as roommates who put up with a casual friend rather than celebrating the joy of an intimate lover. There was a pulling apart and drifting away where passion gave way to passive complacency. As with fault lines, they can expand little by little. A husband and wife may see the shift at the beginning of a rift. But here are a few telltale statements of isolation that leads to separation:

- I feel like there's no pleasing you. No matter what I do, it bothers me when you are critical.
- Why should I even try anymore? We've had this discussion already, let's talk about it later.
- I don't know how to get inside his mind. He's isolated and won't communicate with me.
- She's always on her phone. Rarely wants to be intimate and is always in a snappy mood.
- Let's just let it go, and maybe it'll work itself out.
- I don't have the problem, you do. Why don't you deal with it yourself?

Thrust Faults

Thrust faults are blocks that *slide* one on top of the other. Imagine two pieces of land colliding. One has the will to dominate the other. This is how the Rocky Mountains were formed. The goal in marriage should be unity rather than dominance. Instead, as couples fight for power, striving to prove the other wrong, or devaluing their partner's opinion, they thrust themselves over the other. Creating a rocky relationship filled with power struggles.

Drawing a line in the sand to force a perspective over your partner will lead to problems. Should your spouse disagree with the rules you impose in your relationship, the divide can leave them feeling threatened. When you don't see eye to eye, and don't want things to go the way you see as best, when they reject your ideas, you can interpret them as dismissing you. As a result, you may wrestle with feeling invalidated, unsupported, or on some levels, unloved. When these issues remain unaddressed, future disagreements are like squirts of lighter fluid on a persisting flame. After a while, it's not really about why they disagree with you. It's the mere fact of being out of sync with your perspective that you find unacceptable.

With every personality clash, minor disagreement, or parenting struggle encountered, there's a potential fault. We believe that marriage fights of all types are like the buildings shaking as a result of fault lines within the heart. What typically happens is that we survive a quake from the past, but our current friction is the resulting aftershock.

Since time continues to tick, we're forced to move forward, but time won't heal the wounds. So, although you have moved on, you may be increasing the length of an undetected fault line. In essence, we're moving forward with baggage, and it's only a matter of time before your spouse rubs you the wrong way, and the earthquakes begin again.

Emotional trauma may be triggered in your relationship if you've lived through, or are experiencing something like the following examples:

- Feeling as if your necessities aren't being taken care of. Living with bullying, negligence, verbal or physical abuse.
- Being shut down in instances where you share emotions and long to be understood. Your spouse may reject your attempts saying something like, "you're too emotional."

- Being questioned concerning your memory, judgment, or being manipulated.
- Suppressing parts of yourself out of fear for your spouse's reaction.
- Getting stuck in reoccurring situations that you feel you can't manage.

As you can imagine, the ripple effects of relational trauma vary greatly. Trust can erode. The sense of safety is disrupted, stress is intensified, and good people find themselves stuck in a rut that they can't figure out how to escape. To help you recognize the impact of relational trauma, we've listed a few examples of the effects on the mind and body:

- A heightened sense of feeling unsafe around other people. Almost living with constant suspicion. In some instances, people become nervous or restless in a triggered state. Even beginning to believe you already know that people perceive you in a negative light.
- Physically, it can create digestive issues, migraines, head-aches—even dissociation. An example of this is driving your usual route to your child's daycare center...but on autopilot. You were so numb as a result of stressors that you arrived there, but don't remember the details of actually driving there.
- Trauma can cause increased anxiety or depression.
- Often a sense of shame can arise in people who've been vic-timized by someone close to them.
- Sometimes, we'll isolate ourselves from those closest to us. One might even resist intimacy, both sexually and emotionally.
- It can cast a constant cloud over your head. It's hard to feel joy within yourself or with others around you.
- So how do we avoid earthquakes and aftershocks altogether?

We start by mending the faults in our hearts. We ultimately need healing to reassert the miracle of unity that is marriage. Becoming one and moving together as one rather than rubbing against, falling beneath, or rising above one another. The good news is you are not alone in the mending process. Psalm 34:18 says, "The LORD is close to the brokenhearted; he rescues those whose spirits are crushed." God is readily available to heal and restore your heart. He will give you the ability to love your spouse unconditionally through any transition.

You can't heal a wound by saying it's not there. You can only heal what you're willing to confront. The good news is that with marriage, unlike earthquakes, we can do something to prevent the shaking of our foundations. We can stop the tremors altogether and mend the fault in our hearts. That's what this book is all about.

Hope for the Future

You may be reading this, and it may be a bit overwhelming to realize that your marriage needs healing from the trauma of some tough transitions. Please know that you're not the only one. On some level, every couple has dealt with some form of friction due to division below the surface. If you've experienced earthquakes in your relationship, I want you to be encouraged. God gives beauty for ashes and restoration in the aftermath of devastation.

As we write this book, we're on a mountain top surrounded by trees and calming springs. On our way up, we drove through winding roads and weaved within the walls of a cliff. It's so magnificent to see the layers of rock beneath the trees. This mountain is the result of landmasses that violently clashed. Pressing into one another until it formed what we stand amazed by today.

You see, the past can either make you *bitter* or it can make you *better.* Our goal is to show you how to shake off the trauma after the transition. Because new life can grow from the fertile soil of your pain. When your hearts are healthy, you can overcome the past and move forward as a fruitful family with a successful future.

And by the way, the couple who permitted us to share their story were able to find healing and grew stronger after enduring earthquakes and tremors. On that dark day by the lake, she found a church on a nearby property. She shared what she was feeling to a community counselor who happened to be there that day. After praying over her, the counselor called her husband, who then came to pick her up and take her home. Shame began to rise within as she admitted to what she'd genuinely felt for so long but hadn't told him. After taking it all in, he felt betrayed and shut out of her world. But after many difficult, vulnerable conversations, they put everything on the table and addressed their fault lines together. Leading them to reach out for professional help. And after speaking with their OBGYN and seeing a prenatal/postpartum therapist, she began to work through solutions to balance hormones. And he was more sensitive to her needs, intentionally asking questions about her wellbeing and becoming a better listener. They were able to find their voice both separately and as a healthy family of three.

We must realize that we are navigating life as ever-changing individuals undergoing continual changes, and collisions are bound to happen. In the next chapter, we'll dive deeper into the world of transitions, and its effects on our behavior as we move forward in our relationships.

CHAPTER TAKEAWAYS

1. Can you identify transitions within your marriage and see how its effects mirror the aftermath of an earthquake?

2. Let's take this a little deeper and compare the "fault lines" to your situation. Which fault does your transition parallel?

   a. Strike-slip faults - You've gone on strike and have reached a relational impasse.

   b. Normal faults - Dysfunctional behavior has become the norm resulting in separation and distrust.

   c. Thrust faults - Couples fight for power, striving to prove the other wrong.

3. We talked about how a response to transitions can be in the form of isolation. Have you and your spouse dealt with isolation?

2

Face Morphing

"Before you marry a person you should
first make them use a computer with slow
Internet to see who they really are."

—WILL FERRELL

LAST YEAR, WE ENTERTAINED THE LATEST SOCIAL MEDIA trend—a face morphing app— that took center stage. Here's how it worked: you upload a recent snapshot, the app does its magic, and poof! You've aged by 50 years. It was frightening to behold some of our friend's future selfies. Overall, it was a cool and funny glimpse into a possible future. Face morphing apps tend to awaken us to the fragility of time and the reality of change. Searching curiously to see the potential changes in our faces. But it is not just what we share of ourselves, but also the sheer joy that comes with laughing at or picking apart our friend's faces.

Humans are experts at critically analyzing images. We instinctively judge one another and find faults. Especially in those we're closest to. Mostly because our familiarity creates mental snapshots of what we want them to be. Should they deviate from our expectations, let the disappointment begin. Jesus gave a great revelation on this very subject. He said in Luke 6:41-42,

> *"It's easy to see a smudge on your neighbor's face and be oblivious to the ugly sneer on your own. Do you have the nerve to say, 'Let me wash your face for you,' when your own face is distorted by contempt? It's this I-know-better-than-you mentality again, playing a holier-than-thou part instead of just living your own part. Wipe that ugly sneer off your own face and you might be fit to offer a washcloth to your neighbor"* (MSG).

I have to admit that I'd spent a lot of time being a self-righteous critic of my wife's snapshot. Especially in seasons where she was in the process of changing from the familiar version of the person I came to love. After twenty-two years, I can say that I've seen her change a lot in our time together. Looking back now, I can see that I wanted a sense of control over who she was becoming, especially as she related to me. Due to my immaturity and selfish nature, I'd get frustrated within the morphing of her personality. As she was becoming, I was begrudging. Ironically what I couldn't see was that from her perspective, I was changing as well. And she was putting up with me during my stages of metamorphosis.

Yes, there were many times that I, Lanette, was frustrated with Sean's process regarding personality adjustments. In fact, the more controlling he became, the more I retreated within. I couldn't deal with my metamorphosis, his issues, and his controlling behaviors. Something had to give and at times it was me. Giving in, compromising, and shutting down pieces of my personality to "keep the peace." I've come to realize, this wasn't a healthy routine. Building walls to shield your true self to satisfy the weaknesses in others enables their dysfunctional behavior. So, while you're seeking personal growth, you simultaneously opt out of living within the prison of your personality.

My "I know better than her, holier-than-thou" moments kept us trapped in a cycle of going tit for tat. When we should've given more room and patience during the transitions of the soul, we would argue with one another as a result of offending their inconsistencies. I'm not referring here to being offended merely by mistakes made. But more so the below the surface root causes of the earthquakes. Frustrations bred from a transition of personality.

The truth is that none of us are static beings. We're complicated, ever-changing, and multidimensional at the same time. The challenge for couples is to find joy in their transformations, rather than contempt as we observe their evolution.

Two-faced and Then Some

Have you ever heard of the term "two-faced?" When I was growing up, if someone called you two-faced, it was an insult. They were calling you dishonest, phony, or somehow disingenuous. Where I'm from, those were fighting words!

While studying the Hebrew word for "face" in the Bible, I found an eye-opening truth. "Paniym" is a plural noun meaning "face." It expresses the motion of our many moods, emotions, and thoughts. All of the different movements reflected in the face. It represents an individual's wholeness of being. This is teaching us that everyone has not only two faces, but many many more.

If your spouse's faces, moods, emotions, and thoughts make you uncomfortable, consider what they're facing with you. Ultimately, we're all multi-faced, so learning to love your spouse, even while they're transitioning faces, is the key. In these volatile moments, they need unconditional love and support. Constant criticism is counterproductive and slows positive change. And they may change into another face you didn't want to see.

You can love them, but not like everything about them.

Our youngest daughter loves spaghetti but hates onions. There was a time I would try to persuade her to eat the onions, hoping that she'd enjoy them one day as much as I did. Nineteen years later, she still doesn't like onions. Instead of forcing her to conform, I began to cut them larger so that she could love the dish but pick out the onions that she doesn't like. Within your marriage, you must learn to love the dish as a whole, while disliking a few things that come with it.

Embracing the Faces of the Soul

When signing up for marriage, we commit to love them with a six-pack to no-pack at all. From gray hair, all the way to little to none left. Loving them when their makeup is on, and when it's off. Love them always, but strive to make them feel it, especially while they're in processing—while they're finding themselves after or during a transition, can be difficult both for them and you.

In many ways, our sense of self comes from our connections to others. In some cases, our identity is attached to what we do or how well we're performing in life. Essentially, we are always in processing.

For instance, I, Lanette, needed to have major surgery. At that time, our children were under the age of 6. Sean's role had to morph from a spouse to a full-time caregiver, a personal chef, and a parent. As a husband, he was being stretched to take on unforeseen responsibilities. Our routine was challenged. The tension caused us physical exhaustion for different reasons. Emotionally I was drained, and he was mentally overwhelmed with the new adjustment of life.

We typically see ourselves according to what we do. "I am an entrepreneur" or "I'm a nurse." The title almost functions as the definition of who we are. Imagine then transitioning from a career that's become one of your many faces. Maybe there were layoffs, you had to move to a new city, or you've retired. Your sense of self has taken a hit. This may cause trauma within your relationship because the framework of their identity has been altered to some extent. If you're the spouse who's walking with them through this career change, you may notice a difference in how they treat you. It may leave you feeling some kind of way. But their inconsistent treatment towards you, their distant behavior, or even forgetfulness towards you may be the result of a transition within them.

If you find yourself saying or feeling things like: I don't know who you are anymore, We've fallen out of love, I don't want to be around them, I'm not attracted to them anymore, I don't respect them; It's an indicator that you're seeing or have seen something about them that's clouding the good things you once knew to be true. You may have what is called **face blindness.**

Face blindness is a cognitive disorder of face perception where the ability to recognize familiar faces is impaired, although other aspects of visual processing and intellectual functioning remain intact. I know this sounds strange, but it's a real thing. And I'm not making this up. When someone has it, they can see a person in front of them, but can't connect the dots of who they've known them to be.

It reminds us of so many couples we've counseled over the years. Let's say, for example, a husband lost his job. That's a "Little T" transition. But here's where the tremors kick in. During his job search, his wife notices he's playing the video game for hours while awaiting callbacks from online applications. From her perspective, his behavior is passive and maybe even uncaring. The fate of the family finance is in jeopardy as he's gaming away on the couch. What's happening for her is that she sees one of his many faces. She may call this face Mr. Passive, and it's a complete turnoff.

Perhaps on occasion, incidents transpired, and your spouse didn't tell you the truth? That breach of trust may cause an internal fracture within you. You subconsciously overlay an untrustworthiness over them. So, even though they made a mistake in one area, there's a cloud of distrust that blinds you of their positive qualities.

Have you reached a moment where your sex drives fell out of sync? Is it the result of hormonal changes, or is there another motivating force? While trying to process why they're less intimate sexually while you're in desperate need, you may feel rejected. Leading you to see another face on them that you may label "unloving."

There are so many scenarios that I could point to, but I think you get the idea. You find a fault in them, and it creates a fault line within you. Some event occurs, and you've seen a different side of them. A smear on their face, and just like that, here comes face blindness. Where you can recognize their dirt, but you can't dig through the worst of them to uncover the gold within them.

Their face, for whatever reason, has changed, and you don't see the best of them. It may be difficult to separate what they've done with who they are at their core. You must know and honestly believe that there's still good within them. Find your way back to loving them despite their flaws. In the moments of face blindness, ask God to restore your sight. To help you see them through His eyes of grace. Then agree with, and speak over them, His revealed truth rather than criticism.

This is huge: Your criticisms may very well be rooted in the facts, but it may also perpetuate the very thing you wish to prevent. If you're accusing your spouse or consistently finding faults, your words may behave like self-fulfilling prophecies. It is compounding the interest of a false narrative. When a season of weakness or momentary lapse in judgment get resurfaced and tossed into their face, it's hard to escape.

Isaiah 43:19 says, *"For I am about to do something new. See, I have already begun! Do you not see it? I will make a pathway through the wilderness. I will create rivers in the dry wasteland."*

If your relationship has been in a dry place, God can create rivers of refreshing. In the moments where you can't see the way, He provides pathways to breakthrough. There's a new thing available if you're willing to forget the old stuff. You may say, "Well, you don't know my situation." You're right, I don't know all the details, but God does. My question to you, "Is there anything too hard for God?"

Maybe today is the day to release the past so that you may begin to grab hold of present promises for your family's hope and future. Every day you have to make a conscious decision to manage your expectations and face the facts of life with God's truth. Begin to call out the gold in them. Affirming their positive qualities, speak to strengths, and encourage the greatness within them. Call out of them the precious from beneath their imperfections.

Studies have shown that positive affirmation decreases health-deteriorating forms of stress. It can increase physical performance. As well as help us to perceive otherwise "threatening" messages with less resistance. It even improves overall academic achievements.[3]

Leena S. Guptha DO in embodied wellness writes:

"Affirmations with words and valuable phrases can be quite powerful, imprinting positive messages in our subconscious mind. These affirmations can help with rewriting the thoughts in the files, where often negative messages that originate from a repeated phrase can be stored. The only barrier to achieving our personal goals is ourselves. We often need to retrain our thought patterns to see the joys, opportunities, and possibilities in life rather than the limitations.

---

3. Catherine Moore, "Positive Daily Affirmations: Is There Science Behind It?," (PositivePsychology.com). https://positivepsychology.com/daily-affirmations/.

Our thoughts can drive our attitudes, our actions, and our behaviors. We can use this powerful chain reaction for empowerment, achievement, success, and self-actualization."[4]

Your spouse needs your support when they're at their worst. We're not saying to live in denial. Nor suggesting you won't have to confront some relational issues that bother you along the way. We are saying that before you do, try applying positive reinforcement rather than criticizing your mate into better shape.

How Do We Overcome the Transition of Faces?

Become super-recognizers: Super-recognizers are people with significantly better-than-average face recognition ability. Super recognizers have the ability to memorize and recall thousands of faces, often having seen them only once.

Seeing your spouse through the lens of grace provides super recognition. "Well, how do I do that?" Well, you perceive them as Jesus does towards you. You don't earn his love with good behavior. Neither do you lose your relationship with God when you make mistakes. He doesn't kick you out of the house or make you sleep on the Heavenly couch when you've made mistakes. He sees into your heart, knows all the realities of your flaws, and still accepts you in as His own, unconditionally.

Another way to become a super-recognizer is to serve them as you would serve Jesus if you met him in the flesh. Treat them as if they were Jesus' very own body. Now you may be thinking, "Wait a minute now, that's taking it too far. My spouse ain't perfect, and I won't treat them just like Jesus." But, let me show you straight from the Bible that this is the standard expectation:

4. Leena S. Guptha, DO "To Affirm or Not Affirm?" Psychology Today (Sussex Publishers, LLC). https://www.psychologytoday.com/us/blog/embodied-wellness/201704/affirm-or-not-affirm.

"Then the King will say to those on his right, 'Enter, you who are blessed by my Father! Take what's coming to you in this kingdom. It's been ready for you since the world's foundation. And here's why: I was hungry and you fed me, I was thirsty and you gave me a drink, I was homeless and you gave me a room, I was shivering and you gave me clothes, I was sick and you stopped to visit, I was in prison and you came to me.'" "Then those 'sheep' are going to say, 'Master, what are you talking about? When did we ever see you hungry and feed you, thirsty and give you a drink? And when did we ever see you sick or in prison and come to you?' Then the King will say, 'I'm telling the solemn truth: Whenever you did one of these things to someone overlooked or ignored, that was me—you did it to me'" (Matthew 25:34–40 MSG).

The proof of concept here is pretty clear. While giving an account of how we cared for people, Jesus' explanation of how He views our treatment of one another is astonishing. When our love is mercifully generous towards others, He sees those we help as if we're helping Him directly. He interprets kindness shown to others personally.

Now, if this passage emphasizes serving the people we don't know as a service to God himself, how much more important is it that we do the same for our spouse? Here's the picture of just how important it is to God.

Wives, understand and support your husbands in ways that show your support for Christ. The husband provides leadership to his wife the way Christ does to his church, not by domineering but by cherishing. So just as the church submits to Christ as he exercises such leadership, wives should likewise submit to their husbands. Husbands, go all out in your love for your wives, exactly as Christ did for the church—a love marked by giving,

*not getting. Christ's love makes the church whole. His words
evoke her beauty. Everything he does and says is designed to
bring the best out of her, dressing her in dazzling white silk, radi-
ant with holiness. And that is how husbands ought to love their
wives. They're really doing themselves a favor—since they're
already "one" in marriage* (Ephesians 5:22–28 MSG).

Here again, we find the calling of sacrificial love towards one
another as a service to God. Since we are one, let's bring out the best
in one another. Husbands, lead with love in the same manner Jesus
sacrificially did for the church, His bride. Wives, supporting your
husband, shares your support for Christ. These are powerful illustra-
tions of the high honor and responsibility of the marriage covenant.
For you to love on this level, you must operate from a place of grace.

Is Your Marriage Stuck in Law or Strong in Love?

In the book of Leviticus, the law of Moses is revealed to Israel.
Following these rules gets complicated, to say the least. Six hundred
and thirteen specific requirements were handed down to the people,
with blessings attached for obeying and consequences for breaking
them. As you can imagine, trying to live out the Levitical law was like
walking on eggshells. One misstep and some devastating outcome
was coming your way.

One section that came to mind while writing this chapter on face
morphing was that there were specific laws regarding skin issues. If
they contracted any type of boil, burn, or rash they'd get labeled as
unclean. Once discovered, a person would show themselves to the
priest, and then they'd kick them out the camp. They'd be quaran-
tined based on the evaluation of their exterior appearance. Can you
imagine what it's like to be removed from those you love because
you've got a skin rash?

Well, during personality transitions, our faces morph into something else. In the context of the soul, sometimes, we morph into someone else. Honestly, consider what life would be like if we didn't change for the better with time. Just as our bodies age over time and we maintain a sense of recognition, but we definitely don't look exactly the same. We age, mature, adapt. We change.

Don't penalize your spouse during the process of their transformation. Love and serve them throughout their variations. As with the law, some marriages operate similarly. One spouse acts as the priest while their mate has a rash that's come to the surface. Some flaw, bad habit, something you find detestable, has become visible on the surface. Now the priest (the spouse) makes external evaluations of their behavior to determine whether they're clean or unclean, whether they can stay in the camp or go into a quarantined-time-out.

Judgment dictates a sentence that says, you're still in the house *but* on punishment. Seen now, according to their sick face, as if that's all they are or have ever been. Such behavior captures what a performance-based marriage displays precisely. When your love swings on the pendulum of performance, it's conditional.

If someone's relationship is rooted in love, their flaws are evident, but you also know that's not *all* they are. The sum total of their character isn't calculated on their worst behavior. Acceptance isn't based on what they do, but rather who they are to you—choosing to value the person rather than their performance.

Now, saying, "I love you" is different from saying, "I love all the things you do." However, it should convey, "While you're becoming all that God created you to be, I'm committed to walking with you. I'm dedicating my life to cheering you on as you transition to a better version of yourself." People who love in this manner devote to others what they're fully aware they'll one day need in return. Every living soul desperately needs unconditional love as they navigate the transitioning between their many faces.

One of the most powerful statements you can declare over your spouse is this: "I see you and I realize you are not the mistakes you've made. Your perfection is not required for my love. I'll love you, even where you're broken. I know God has a future and a hope for you, so I'm walking with you until you get there."

Pledging devotion in this manner truly expresses your oneness. We are sharing successes and even challenges as a team. As they confront issues, their challenge becomes a shared dynamic. They are no longer viewed as "his" problems and "her" dilemma. Without exception, we tackle threats to the team together. And that means WE are in the process of changing.

Discovering the root causes of a person's character flaws makes loving someone on this level a little easier. Unearthing the motives behind the many faces, finding the origins broadens our understanding. In the next chapter, we will help you discover ways to build unity as a couple to move past pain and embrace their process of change during the transition.

CHAPTER TAKEAWAYS

1. Discuss what moods, emotions, or behaviors your spouse is expressing that may be bothering you? How could you communicate this to them in the right way?

2. If you're the one who's changing, what emotions or behaviors are you expressing? How could this affect your spouse?

3. What can you do this week, to show your spouse you love and support them? In other words, *"How can you serve them like Jesus"*?

THREE PATHWAYS TO UNIFY YOUR MARRIAGE

3

Lost in Transition

"I wish that science, if there is a science, would come up with a brain ride where you could take a ride in someone's brain where you could see all their thoughts, and their memories and why they do the things they do and why they feel the way they feel, and I know there's a low-tech version of this just called listening... this would be so much... easier."

—MARIA BAMFORD, THE SPECIAL SPECIAL SPECIAL!

IN EARLY 2001, WE PACKED UP OUR TWO TODDLERS, ALL WE owned, and moved from Indianapolis to Fort Worth, Texas. We transitioned into what we believed would be an opportunity to grow into the life we'd dreamed of with our young family. We were laser-focused on our careers from the moment we hit the road on this new venture. And the more we pressed the gas toward our goals, the more our business and personal lives were intertwined. Though our drive propelled our family forward, it left behind a pile of debris from perpetual power struggles.

Since we were together from our late teens with three children, we had to lean into our careers while trying to deepen our reasonably new relationship.

Lanette and I were highly committed to our toddlers while working in a stringent administrative role. But upon leaving work, we still felt the pressure of trying to meet the demands of taking care of the kids and home. Sean ran his recording studio while leading worship as an associate pastor and also worked full time as a construction supervisor. Upon getting off work, in the time he had for me, there was very little energy. By the time he arrived home, his daily word quotient was pretty much used up. Meanwhile, I was desperately in need of the adult conversations we once shared, you know, before real life kicked in.

We were both shaped by our experiences growing up. Having experienced financial difficultly, we desperately wanted to build a wealthy culture and avoid poverty. Subsequently, we were driven by a fear of failure. Initially, things were ok, but over the next few years, Lanette began to retreat internally to process the trauma of neglect from me. Meet her at one of our marriage events now, and you'll see an outspoken extrovert. But back then, she'd suppressed so much of herself. Upon suffering professional setbacks within the company, we moved to a new city, disappointment kicked in, and financial struggles became a reality.

By the time Lanette mustered up the courage to share her thoughts, I had listened defensively. I couldn't hear beyond my wounded ego. After all, she wasn't the only one in the struggle. I interpreted her cries for help as complaints about my poor performance. As time progressed, I felt weighed down by the pressures of the job and the criticism coming from the home.

Both of us realized that we found our leisure time before having children more fulfilling. Though we loved our time with our kiddos, we desperately needed to find one another again. But we couldn't afford time away from work. Our marriage was going up in flames fast. To say we needed intervention is an understatement. We now realize we needed both Jesus and therapy. To our credit, though, we continued to push through setbacks and disappointments to keep our family together.

To say that we were frustrated is a subtlety. Mentally exhausted and desperate for a solution in both our professional and personal lives, we lost ourselves in the transition process. In our case, work was attached to our identity. We equally desired to work ambitiously, and yet we were longing for a healthy home. We wanted to attain economic freedom while enjoying a successful marriage.

What took place throughout several major transitions was a loss of both individual and shared identity. Remember our definition of transition: *a time when partners are united in the process of changing from one state to another.* So many decisions were made between us and with each one came a level of responsibility that tested the "partners united." In many ways, we became a house divided.

From the moment we decided to relocate to a new city, I, Lanette, made a personal sacrifice to follow Sean's lead in pursuit of his calling. When we made commitments to work a few more hours on the job or take on new clients at the studio—we simultaneously sacrificed extraordinary amounts of attention away from each other. The two of us needed to work things out. Instead, it was as if life was happening to us, and we were clinging on desperately! Now, we realize that we are influential people—the decisions we make as a couple express that power. And the consequences can either build-up or dissolve the integrity of our relationship.

While juggling multiple responsibilities, I, Lanette, neglected personal desires, and suppressed my dreams. I don't regret doing ministry or caring for my children, but I shouldn't have spent years ignoring myself. I allowed transitions of life to separate me from dreams within my heart. As a result, when I finally looked up and asked myself "who I was," it was hard for me to identify. For instance, as the kids grew up, I became a problem solver rather than parenting according to an established purpose from within. So, as they matured and I had fewer problems to solve, it made me question my significance. I was honestly feeling like a failure as a mom. Beyond a doubt, I connected my parenting to my identity instead of parenting out of my identity. The greatest opposition to maximizing our potential, lies within us. It's the battle that lies at the level of our core of our beliefs.

Looking back over how things stacked up, we didn't have much guidance as a couple. No one taught us how to make decisions for our family as one unit rather than single individuals. No one gave us tips on how to avoid earthquakes and mend our fault lines. The target in this chapter is to help *you* work together as a *team*. To offer a more inclusive approach to leading in the moments when life aspirations and family collide. A critical thought to keep in mind is that our perception guides our experience. How we perceive ourselves and our spouse has the power to alter the decisions that we make and the paths we take. Discovering the best way forward calls for processes that help clarify our aspirations, fears, past, and future. As we discuss the three pathways to unity, you'll learn a method that'll bring clarity from the core.

Three Pathways to Unity:

1. The Path of Humility: Humble Yourself to Hear Your Spouse's Heart

C. S. Lewis once said, "Humility is not thinking less of yourself, it's thinking of yourself less." My friends, you're most powerful when you're remarkably humble. The more that couples fight for control, the more they'll lose themselves to pride in the process. Pride manifests in many ways, but ultimately, it shifts blame. No matter what, a self-centered person sees others as the problem. Rarely making concessions for their spouse, they avoid accountability for their actions. In chapter one, we discussed thrust faults where one exerts their will to dominate the other. Here's a thought to consider: God Himself respects our right to choose. He doesn't force Himself or His will on us. While a wife or husband forces their views, opinions, or will on their spouse, whatever results attained in the process inevitably lead to an earthquake. People are designed to pursue freedom. We will fight to gain what we perceive to be an escape from control or bondage. It's similar to the fight or flight response that kicks in during a perceived threat.

If your behavior towards your spouse is perceived by them as manipulative or domineering, they may retreat into themselves as a protective measure. In which case, their assumed despondence may provoke an extrovert who tries to force a response in a situation. As they intensify the conversation, the other person is internally running further and further away to escape both the confrontation and their spouse.

If you want their full participation, you must create a safe space to communicate your hopes, concerns, and desires. This is the best way to begin the process of facilitating unity. Set aside time to hear each other out. This is especially important during transitional moments. Pause to explore what's really going on. In the next chapter, we provide a list of questions and techniques that'll help with this process. Upon hearing one another's answers, couples can grow stronger without losing their goals.

Absorbing this, why would you set a time to hear someone whom you consider inferior in understanding? If you perceive them to be incompetent, why seek their input? This is where humility kicks into high gear. You aren't greater than them. It shouldn't be a competition to win a point. The moment this happens, they lose. Which means the relationship is losing. And you aren't learning much when you're the one who's always talking.

You'll know that you're walking in humility when you put the needs of your spouse above your own. When you've had a hard day's work, are craving a remote in your hand, and want nothing more than to be laid out on the couch with the TV on, but realize your wife has had a hard day, you humble yourself. Run her bath water, put the kids to bed, and make sure that she gets the night off. Humility is on full display when she recognizes that he's a little rusty on his romance game. Still, it's been a while since they've been sexually intimate. He walks into the bedroom and to his surprise...oh yes, humility.

Couples who walk the path of humility honor one another's strengths, but also share their weaknesses. They don't have to have it together all twenty-four-hours of the day. She's able to admit that she gets it wrong sometimes. He can ask forgiveness for forgetting to pay the bill and is willing to admit that the late fee is his fault. The need to be chronically correct has been put in check. In this house, they can be naked and not ashamed. Accepted for who they are because they both realize they're flawed individuals who need one another.

They carry themselves with an open-minded attitude. They ask their spouse questions like, "What do you think we should do about little Billy's bad attitude at school?" Or, "These interest rates are super low, I think right now is the time to buy. Can we pray about the next step?" There's a level of satisfaction and contentment acquired only through the path of humility. Healthy couples are mature enough to see that it's not just about me, but it's about **we**.

Another sure-fire test to determine where you're walking in humility is the ability to forgive your spouse when they get it wrong. Forgiveness means to release the need to get even with them. They don't owe you anything for the crime they've committed against you. It's saying, "I let it go, and I'm completely over it." Are you keeping a scorecard of offense? Holding on to memories of missed opportunities? It's time to let it go. Keep in mind the fact that you've made *plenty* of mistakes. We all desperately need grace, so give as much mercy as you long to receive when they need it most.

2. The Path of Values: Making Value-based Decisions

A powerful game-changer for us was shifting from surface-level fights to substantive dialogue over core beliefs. Advancing beyond nit-picky debates and anxiety-inducing arguments. To cut to the heart of the matter, examining the conflicts emerging from the very core of who we are. In studying our suppressed internal longings, it shifted our perception and priorities. Values are addressed when the right questions are examined in a safe atmosphere with designated time for consideration. (To discover your values, visit SeanandLanette.com)

Comparing stat lines of the most chores completed or which one of you is the parent of the month won't change things on a fundamental level. But couples who attempt to connect to understand and process their emotions behind their decisions manage to make real progress. As they uncover the motives behind their feelings, prioritized choices get made. Pathways that they both agree on will be taken. Building from this foundation of shared unity creates a bond that holds you together. Should things fail to turn out exactly as planned, since it wasn't a one-person decision forced on the other, neither person points fingers. This wasn't a guilt-driven choice rooted in manipulation, so it's just *our* mistake. We can bounce back from what we've learned. When there's clarity at the core level, then the practical decisions fall into place. They also don't make or break the relationship.

Let's say you're in need of making a significant career move, and you're newly married and adjusting as a blended family. The process of discovering your values is critical. Since your values vary, identifying them is the first step. Then there must be negotiation and prioritization. Negotiate your schedule, the budget, and decisions around your values.

Once your values are established, you can set them as priorities. From your business life to family commitments, you'll meet one another's deepest needs. This eliminates the cracks within the crust, and you'll move forward together as one rather than clashing.

3. The Path of Negotiation: Negotiate the Terms of the Agreement and Then Proceed as Partners

This, my friends, is the hard, but necessary work required to accomplish your shared goals. Begin by clearly capturing what you really want as an individual regarding your specific circumstance. Prior to presenting your perspective to your spouse, jot down the specifics of what you desire and give a few reasons why. Then your spouse has an equal opportunity to do the same. But it's important to note that when you're walking the pathway of negotiation, you communicate reasons rather than arguments or justifications. Why? Well, you're not out to prove them wrong for one. Also, you realize the goal isn't to squeeze everything you can out of the deal. You're not working to tip the scales in your favor or trying to score a fair exchange for services rendered. Your building your marriage together and winning together is the only real team triumph. Having heard both sides, you collaborate until you've reached an agreeable course of action. And action is key in light of the conversation. When talks fail to convert to a collaborative effort, it tends to frustrate at least one, if not both partners, in the relationship. At some point, you have to do more than aim at the target; someone's got to pull the trigger.

As you practice collaborative negotiation, try to avoid making major life decisions based on temporary circumstances. In some instances, it's not even the circumstances that are temporary, but rather our emotions. Quick reactions may result in long-term regret. Breathe, take your time, and give space to process. Impulsive choices often lead to a compromise of ethical behavior and a lack of self-control. So as much as its within your power to do so, pause to process. And make sure your plans are in alignment with your values. A few high caliber decisions that qualify are: Which city will we live in next? What's our parenting strategy? How will we divide chores? How much time will we spend with in-laws? What's the best way to respond to this crisis? Should we see a marriage counselor? Is this the best church for our family?

Making essential judgment calls that'll have a lasting impact requires negotiation and agreement. To clear the path for deliberation, set these decisions on a higher level than automated daily choices. These require a level of focus and designated time for consideration.

One mistake we made along the way was taking on the role of being firefighters. Trying to resolve each issue as it arose. That was problematic in that our choices led to actions outside of our shared vision and values. Successful couples make decisions on solid foundations. After humbling themselves and asking the right questions, they negotiate and form a merger to move forward. The two agree on not only the destination but also on a plan to arrive where they're headed. Ask yourself in these moments: What are our boundaries? Did we count up the actual cost? Are we both contributing to the course we'll travel collectively?

Moving forward without common ground will most likely lead to issues along the way. The process of negotiating helps navigate life's difficult choices until you've reached the place of agreement. If you don't tap into the core, then later on in transitions, the cycles of a dysfunctional merger will hinder your growth.

As you can see, we made a lot of mistakes. But through traveling the pathways to unity, we remain committed regardless of what comes our way. Keep in mind that inner healing is a continual

journey and not a destination. Once you master one level, we guarantee another season of change awaits around the corner. But when
you build on your values, you won't lose yourself in the process of
transition.

CHAPTER TAKEAWAYS

We mentioned three pathways to unity. Under each pathway discuss a small step you can take to start the journey.

1. The Path of Humility: Humble yourself to hear your spouse's heart.

2. The Path of Values: Identity your values, then proceed to make decisions.

3. The Path of Negotiation: Negotiate the terms of agreement, then move forward together.

4

Finding the Gold

*"Constant kindness can accomplish much. As the sun
makes ice melt, kindness causes misunderstanding,
mistrust, and hostility to evaporate."*

—ALBERT SCHWEITZER

HAVE YOU EVER AWAKENED TO A SONG STUCK IN YOUR head? One of those moments where the tune becomes an earworm on repeat in your mind. You could describe it as having the singer giving the performance of a lifetime inside your brain. The moment you start repeating their words in your mind, it begins to sound like your voice emanating from you. The moment that you hum their familiar tune, you're under the artist's influence.

As with the melodies stuck in our heads, we are susceptible to being trapped in repeatable life patterns. The Bible refers to these thought patterns in our minds that shape our behaviors as strongholds.

2 Corinthians 10:4 says, *"We use God's mighty weapons, not worldly weapons, to knock down the strongholds of human reasoning and to destroy false arguments."*

Our true identities get boxed in as we sing and consequently believe the lyrics of a lie. During my daughter's choir concert at school, a young lady was singing a solo. Things weren't going well for her, to say the least. She couldn't keep up with the musical accompaniment, she forgot the words, and everyone, including herself, knew the ship was sinking quickly. Suddenly, in a moment of clarity, she abruptly stopped singing the second verse and said, "I'm not doing this!" She then dropped the mic and walked off the stage.

We want to show you how to stop singing along with a lying song! If we don't, then our marriages will be trapped in a cycle of pain from the past. We'll cultivate dysfunctional behaviors and unhappiness. As Lanette and I processed the common denominator of strongholds in our marriage, we realized that our struggle isn't merely what happened to us but also what it did in us. Essentially, how it may have corrupted what we believed of ourselves and one another.

To regain freedom from strongholds over our homes, we've got to recognize the core lies we've believed about one another. Throughout scripture, the kingdom of darkness is on a mission to kill generational legacy, steal our joy, and destroy our families. The greatest weapon in their arsenal are the poisonous lies they whisper about God, ourselves, and one another.

As with the songs stuck in our minds, their accusations become the lyrics we recite within. Eventually, the melody seems as though it's coming from you. Under this deception, the lens that we view God, ourselves, and our spouse through is distorted—leading to entire stretches of seeing life through an unhealthy lens. During which time trust is shattered, hope is diminished, and the marriage of our dreams gets deferred. The decisions we make in a deceived state are rooted in faulty logic. When our perception is off, it creates a chain reaction that's often hard to detect.

A Biblical Illustration in the Art of Deception

When Adam & Eve (the first couple) "Saw that the fruit was good for food" they took, ate, and, as a result, died. But what led them to consume what God clearly said to avoid? Well, the forbidden fruit wasn't the only thing they consumed. They'd also taken a bite into Satan's deception. Let's trace the pattern of core lies:

- Satan: "God is lying to you. He isn't trustworthy. You're better off in this world being your own gods."
- Adam and Eve: "Maybe he's right. God's been withholding the good life from us. Let's eat from the forbidden tree."

We have the advantage of seeing the foolishness of their decision in hindsight. But for a moment, consider why they made such a massive mistake? Their warped belief gave birth to wicked behavior. The truth was made plain to them by God in the beginning. He was right all along. At one point, they lived in truth as their reality. As a result, they avoided the forbidden fruit and were safe. They lived according to God's purpose for their lives and prospered as a result.

But after a conversation with the smooth-tongued devil, they began to favor the allure of the forbidden. They were buying into the possibility that God was withholding His best from them. All the while, they were prospering in the center of paradise. At some point, they began to believe a false narrative of their Creator. Since disconnected from their source of truth, their identities were compromised, and corrupt behavior followed. Just as Adam and Eve's marriage, we face the same dilemma daily— monitoring the lens through which we view reality.

Couples share an identity that's rooted in their accomplishments, failures, upbringing, and experiences. The key to freedom is the way that we see the truth. Strongholds function as negative lenses through which we evaluate our marriage. President and Founder of affairrecovery.com says, "Once that lens is put in place, that belief becomes the underlying theme through which you evaluate the marriage." They filter how you see your spouse and, ultimately, how you treat them. As you process unhealthy thoughts, your core beliefs create a theme. A theme by which you perceive your relationship. This perception drives how you act and react with your family.

These core beliefs act as self-fulfilling prophecies. One man I counseled who actually cheated on his wife, grew angry with her as she seemed cold and isolated. The more he saw her reaction to his infidelity, he treated her in the same manner he perceived her to be. As a result, she felt even more unloved by him. Since he treats her with contempt, she grows cold and distant to protect herself. Do you see the effect our lens can have on our marriage?

Do you believe a false narrative about yourself or your spouse? Choosing to willfully sing along with a lying song. We want to show you how to destroy the strongholds that imprison you and shatter the lies that you've accepted within yourself. Some melodies we've picked up along the way were memorized during traumatic moments. One of the symptoms of trauma is re-experiencing it in various ways, like literal reenactments that recreate a past trauma in your present life. For example, "This is very apparent in children, who play by mimicking what occurred during the trauma, such as by pretending to crash a toy airplane into a toy building after seeing televised images of the terrorist attacks on the World Trade Center of September 11, 2001." [5]

It's Time for a Lens Correction

When our family moved from Texas to North Carolina, we had to find a new optometrist. I, Sean, have always maintained 20/20 vision throughout my life. But while everyone else in our crew was getting fitted for their glasses and contacts, I was feeling left out. Plus, I love the challenge of proving that I can see the smallest letters, so I took a vision test. I read every letter but for the first time in my 40 years of living, it was harder to see the smallest letters. The eye doctor said, "Sean you see everything well, but I suggest you try looking at the eye chart with a slight adjustment." She had me looking through a new lens. In an instant, my 4k vision became 8k. She then informed me that eye muscles weaken over time, and deterioration happens for many people at the age of forty. Here's the thing, I was so used to seeing the world with my "normal" eyesight, but without a new lens, I couldn't realize there was better sight available.

For change to occur, there must be a lens replacement over our hearts to offset the imperfections we see in each other. Imagine viewing your spouse as God does. To know their potential while being fully aware of their problems, and still love them for who they are. To treat them in a way that shows you've truly forgiven them. As if they owe you nothing but love. Here is real passion personified. But if you continuously meditate on their negative traits, you'll be trapped in a prison of offense. Imagine for a moment instead that you're fighting to stay focused on their positive characteristics. You're focused on celebrating their strengths. Not just when you witness them getting

5. Trauma-Informed Care in Behavioral Health Services, Rockville (MD), 2014 (Treatment Improvement Protocol (TIP) Series, No. 57.) Chapter 3, "Understanding the Impact of Trauma." Available from: https://www.ncbi.nlm.nih.gov/books/NBK207191/

it right. When their behavior doesn't quite measure up, they still matter just the same to you, so you speak well of them. Even going so far as to compliment intrinsic value, they fail to recognize within themselves.

There is tremendous power in affirmation. Especially when it comes from someone who's genuinely in your corner. To hear someone laser-focused on appreciating you in this world is a gift. It inspires and builds up rather than critically tearing down. Tapping into the reasons you were drawn to your spouse, to begin with, will help to recall those qualities. Write them down and find ways to add value to your spouse. Call out the gold in them so that they can see it too.

This may be a dramatic shift for you. If you know that you've been consistently critical and your critique is correct, your position must shift. Change from being a *life inspector* to their *loving partner.* You realize that a performance-based relationship is counterproductive. It's exhausting for you to live as a judge and jury. For them, they'll never measure up. That's why a new lens on life is key to your growth as a team. To improve your level of capabilities as a couple begins with healing our perceived identities.

The Way I Perceive You Determines the Way I Treat You

Is your spouse the source of your pain? Does part of you believe they're the reason for a season of unhappiness? Has your tolerance for their incompetence run out? If your responses are less than gracious while living through transitions, pause for a moment, and recalibrate your perspective. Think to yourself: *The way I perceive you determines the way I treat you.*

Is there a moment when you should treat your spouse as an enemy? I know that enemy is a strong word, but here's the definition. *An enemy is a person **actively opposed** or **hostile** to someone.* You shouldn't live as if you're sleeping with the enemy.

If you feel that they're opposed to you, get to the root of why you think this way rather than the 'who' you think it towards in the moment. Who they are is your lover. The reasons for the active opposition may vary. Let's say you're clashing over a lack of help around the house. If they're not contributing to chores, you may be seeing a face that screams 'uncaring.' After all, you've created a neat and tidy environment only to be trashed by a seemingly inconsiderate individual. How often do you have to ask to place dirty clothes in the hamper and not all over the house? Are you feeling under-appreciated because it seems as if your voice isn't being heard?

If you've experienced anything similar to this, I, Lanette, can relate. We went through a transition with our work schedules, the kids were involved in more after-school activities, and the house was an afterthought for everyone except me. I know what it feels like to have everyone in the house focused on other things rather than maintaining the home. You can quickly feel isolated, alone, and you're the only one doing what's necessary.

My desire is a perpetually clean house. However, I was living with unmet expectations, and that was unfair. But this is where we've grown as a family. I no longer live in a prison of frustrations. Breakthrough in this area came as I refused to assume that there was malicious intent. We began to pause to consider the shift in our seasons. There was a transition in the family schedule that left my needs unmet. I was reacting to them while they were responding to the shift.

At one point, Lanette was on edge. Quick-tempered and more intensely asking everyone to help out. As the rest of us reluctantly dragged our feet and half-heartedly caved in to help out, I noticed one day she was visibly upset. I asked her how she felt. Lanette told me she didn't feel as if we were considering her needs and took it as though we didn't care, and in some ways, she was flat out being ignored. Which is totally understandable, and there was truth to it.

But no one in the family lost any love for her. She was still my queen and to the kids, the best mom in the world. It's just that cleaning on the level she desired wasn't our priority. But since she was our priority, it shifted my perspective. That didn't change, however, until we paused to focus on the real problem. We got together and focused on why we were conflicted. We weren't enemies, after all. We simply needed an agreed-upon schedule and delegated assignments. We'd merely failed to adjust after undergoing a transition of more rigorous calendars. We had to come up with who would do what and by what time. Coupled with a rewards system for chores completed and consequences if left uncompleted within a specific timeframe, we were back on track.

We were all experiencing new challenges in our lifestyles. Lanette saw morphed faces from the family. Meanwhile, I was starting to witness the change in her face as well. We had to see each other's value, and once we found the gold, it shaped our vision. But the moment a person is seen as your enemy, you'll instinctively seek justice for crimes committed against you.

If your expectation assumes, "they should have known better," be careful not to allow a knee-jerk reaction of withholding your best because they didn't *qualify* for it. Basically, saying they didn't earn your best because people didn't give you theirs. After all, why reward average attentiveness? Somehow, they have to realize they messed up, right? Am I supposed to just let them get away with it?

No, we're not suggesting a marriage without accountability. But instead, one filled with grace and acceptance of who they are rather than their performance. A works-based relationship will rise and fall to the level of behavior. Seeing as though we're imperfect people, with that as your mantra, you set yourself up for an unstable emotional roller coaster.

We suggest that you realize that you're both very flawed individuals who've chosen to love beyond inherent issues. You commit to serving them as they are, not as you want to **make** them. If there are behaviors, tendencies, or problematic personality traits, focus on the problems without cutting off the person. Just as God does with us individually, we must follow His lead collectively. He gave us sacrificial love before we even knew we needed it. For your spouse, with God's help, commit to showing them love in the same style.

Picture a sick patient who's checked themselves into the ER. They're vomiting all over the place. In this scenario, *you* are the nurse who's assisting them. You're there to serve them and restore them to health. While transporting them, they vomit again. Except, this time, it gets all over you. Do you quit your job? Is that patient your enemy? Do you serve them on the level of your disgust toward their sickness?

Of course not! You continue to help them get well even through the mess they made. Why? It's because you know they're sick. You know they are in your care so that you can help them get well. Instinctively, there's a measure of grace. This doesn't make what they've upchucked smell any better. It's still really gross, and the circumstances are awful. But you just change your scrubs and you get back to work with your fellow nurses, because there's a patient that requires your patience.

How Do I Change the Lens?

Back in the day, photos captured on film were developed over time in a dark room. Photographers had to catch the lighting and background in the moment. If there was a mistake with the original or any of the stages of development in the photo lab, you'd have to start from scratch to get it right.

This generation has 4K photos at the click of the thumb on a smartphone. With these high-quality images, we also have apps that interchange filters over the original photos. Want to doctor acne from the skin to make it appear flawless? No problem. We have the power to manipulate the original image and make it look as we want to see it as opposed to what it truly is.

The challenge with transitions with a changing person is that we may try to doctor the image. Please hear this, any form of manipulation to your spouse will backfire. Don't overlay a filter that makes them more palatable for you. One defense mechanism employed in relationships is projection. It's hard to detect, but it's devastating if not dealt with properly. Projection is when we detach what we don't like about ourselves and attach it to someone else. It's hard to see because it's played out on a subconscious level and usually manifests as a protective mechanism.

When this happens, there's a sense of confidence that our spouse is at fault, and we fail to see our contribution to the collision. In the same way, a bully might cast their feelings or fears on their victim. Blaming and shaming begin to pour out as a result, and this derails intimacy in the aftershock of the earthquake. Couples end up fighting the wrong fights as the epicenter of the faults remains undiscovered.

This is a challenging position for a marriage because your spouse is being accused at a scene where there's been no actual crime. Should you start to question "are you to blame," or "is this their fault?" this may be a cycle that's rooted in projection. Communication is hindered because the conversations aren't rooted in truth, but in a shadow cast by a lie. The relationship gets trapped in a stronghold.

In an article written by Monika Hoyt, she describes the nature of projection:

1. "An example might be that you are attracted to another person outside of your relationship. You have not fully admitted this to yourself. Then you end up accusing your partner of being unfaithful. Really, the desire to be unfaithful lives within you, but you see it in your partner."

2. "Another example could be that your partner accuses you of being selfish because you take time for yourself away from family responsibilities. But your partner has a deep wish for self-care and "escaping" responsibilities. They believe these desires are selfish. Thus, they resent you for taking time for yourself, because they don't." [6]

Before you respond verbally by casting judgment on your spouse, take a moment to process your emotions. If not, you may project your insecurities onto your spouse. It's like dumping seeds of negativity into the ground where none was there before. A great example of this is when your spouse finds you handsome or beautiful, but since you don't see yourself as attractive, you might accuse them of being turned off by you. If this takes place, the relationship functions like a seesaw. One minute you're doing well, and the next is filled with negative thoughts flooding the relationship.

The Power of Release

If there's a running list of past mistakes that's piling up in your mind, you're becoming a judge. The full-time Ebert of your leading actors' performance. What's worse is when you live as a critic of their current film, it's hard to disassociate their past from the present. Our negative biases tend to hop in the driver's seat. Next thing you know, you become the judge of their current body of work, and your memory draws from their previous performances. The power of release is exercised when you're willing to let go of over-analyzing their actions. Retiring from the role of being their number one critic.

Without realizing it, a critical tongue will cut them so deep, they instinctively seek asylum from your verbal assault. Shielding

6. Monika Hoyt, "Projection in Relationships: Stop It from Ruining Your Connection." The Couple's Cure, https://www.monikahoyt.com/projection-in-relationships/.

themselves by tuning you out of their world. Essentially, they become a shell of themselves, for fear of criticism. So, all you'll see is the person you've shaped them to be because they'll only allow the part of them that you've approved of to shine. Now, in order to protect themselves, their personality hides behind the walls of disengagement. And when their partner seeks intimacy, they're emotionally detached and closed for real conversation as they attempt to avoid further criticism. A relationship with critical people is simply draining.

If you're curious as to whether or not you're overly critical, ask yourself the following questions: Do conversations lean towards all the details of what's going wrong? Are crude comments the norm? Are either of you highly judgmental of the other's actions or choices? Is the atmosphere rarely positively charged with compliments or affirmation?

The key to transitioning out of this mindset is to create a culture of compassion. How do you accomplish this? Ask yourself, "What do you appreciate about them?" Make a list of their talents. Jot down positive attributes. Recall how they've been there for you in those moments when their best qualities were on display.

The discipline of daily, positive contributions in replacement of the negative norm is vital. At one time, I, Sean, was a personal trainer. I'd ask my clients what their goals were. Some people would respond, "I want abs," or "I want a beach body with a six-pack." I knew what the phrase implied. Still, the desire for abs is a bit misleading. The truth is that we all come into the world with abs. That's right, you've already got what you've always wanted all along. However, if you can't see your six-pack, it may be hidden beneath layers of adipose tissue, or you can call it...fat. If you want to expose the muscle from beneath, you'll need to put the right fuel in while burning the unhealthy stuff out. Over time, what's been hiding within all along will start shining through, but this takes daily disciple and effort. Healthy food costs a little more money. Exercise is sometimes painful, and you've got to stay consistent to attain lasting results. But my friend, it's worth the investment to become the healthiest version of yourself.

There's a healthy version of your spouse, beneath their evident character flaws. But wouldn't it be wrong to love them more when they arrive in their best shape? Shouldn't they receive the same amount of value and love while they're at their worst as they receive on the way to their best state? It's worth the consistent effort of daily affirmation.

It's harder to affirm a person you believe to be guilty of wrongdoing. Forgiveness is not only mandated by God, but it's a mandatory practice for those who want to move beyond mistakes. Wipe their slate completely clean. You'll know you've forgiven when you've tossed out the need to get even with them for their offensive behavior. You hang up your hat on going tit for tat. You see them as they are rather than all the things that you remember they've done. When people say things like, "I'll forgive, but I'll never forget," it proves that their bent on holding a grudge. But unforgiveness fertilizes the root of bitterness and that will inevitably grow and choke the life out of your future. The Bible says the price, or consequence, of sin is death. That is why Jesus' life was exchanged in sinful mankind's place. When He died on the cross, He killed the power of sin, and to those who trust in Him, it's destructive consequences. The person who carries people's offenses, transgressions, and mistakes within themselves become an incubator of death. They are like fertile ground, holding on to an abnormal growth of stress as a result of them carrying what Jesus killed on the cross. Bearing the full weight of hurt, discord, and brokenness that was delivered when someone failed to treat them properly. The power of release is that it heals you from sleeplessness, seething anger, and torment of your soul. Forgiveness also enlarges peaceable grounds for the relationship to begin repair. There's a oneness with God and those close to you that's renewed as your heart is healed from old wounds. Lewis B. Smedes said, "To forgive is to set a prisoner free and discover that the prisoner was you." Should you fail to forgive, you simultaneously abandon the pathway of love. Harboring resentment prohibits a resolution of the pain.

In *Freedom From Your Past* by Jimmy Evans, he shares The Threefold Process of Genuine Forgiveness. They challenge us to first "Repent to God for unforgiveness." The goal here is to first acknowledge the fact that it is truly wrong to hold onto the sin of others. God, in His graciousness, has completely forgiven us. Who are we then to withhold from others what has been lavishly poured out on us? The second step is to "Release the person from our judgment." Let God handle retribution. Vengeance is the Lord's and His alone to manage. He doesn't need our support in ruling the cosmos. Our personal word choices, negative opinions, and revenge-seeking are unnecessary. Make the decision to release it. We've always taught that you may even have to forgive the same offense against you several times within the same day! As many times as the repetition of the act stirs unhealthy emotions, bat it down again by placing judgment in the hands of The Judge. The third step is tough, but with the help of God, you can do it. "We must bless our offender." Yikes. But the Bible clearly lays out in several passages that this is what's best for those who want to be blessed. Check out Romans 12:14-19:

> *Bless those who persecute you. Don't curse them; pray that God will bless them. Be happy with those who are happy, and weep with those who weep. Live in harmony with each other. Don't be too proud to enjoy the company of ordinary people. And don't think you know it all! Never pay back evil with more evil. Do things in such a way that everyone can see you are honorable. Do all that you can to live in peace with everyone. Dear friends, never take revenge. Leave that to the righteous anger of God. For the Scriptures say, "I will take revenge; I will pay them back," says the LORD.*

The Truth Game

There's gold in your spouse's hills. But you've got dig deep within the mine. We want to challenge you to play a game. It's a tough one initially, especially if you're in a tough season in your marriage. But it's one that'll pay off big in the long run. It's called the truth game. Here's how it works.

Whenever your spouse irks you, makes a mistake, or fails to meet your expectations, find the truth. Find the truth about their innate goodness, beyond the temporary lapse of judgment or failure to hear you after you've called them three times in a row. If their behavior fails to deliver, you need to find the truth. If not, you may begin to accept their temporary error as a forever truth.

This game helps you avoid adopting a catastrophizing mindset. Catastrophizing happens when we assume the worst of a situation or someone. Suppose you've encountered a bad experience with a person or witnessed a disastrous situation that somewhat embeds itself in your mind when facing similar trauma, people, or behavior. In that case, it can act as a trigger for a protective mechanism.

Situations won't improve by assuming the worst. In fact, depression and anxiety may set in due to projections from the unconscious mind. A person can create in their own mind a catastrophe. They imagine a reality that they consequently project onto others. In doing so, they relive the experience over and over again. Imagine your marriage stuck in the worst season because the mindset of the couple won't allow them to break free of worst-case scenarios.

To end the pain of the past, you must release it. But afterward, you must fill the vacancy of the past with a new reality in the present. Otherwise, what's been there previously is a perfect fit because it's so familiar to us. Learn to pause in the moment and find the truth of who they are now. Take a breath and know who you both are in that moment. And with a very logical, rational mind, express what you know to be good and true of them. Ephesians 4:31-32 says,

Get rid of all bitterness, rage, anger, harsh words, and slander, as well as all types of evil behavior. Instead, be kind to each other, tenderhearted, forgiving one another, just as God through Christ has forgiven you.

Speaking the truth realigns and renews your relationship. When you replace the lens of *"the worst things about you are..."* with the lens of *"the best truths about you..."* that's when you mine the gold within. As you discover and affirm the gold within them, you'll get more productivity from your positivity.

Your words can add value and produce healing or tear down and poison. If all that flows from you is negative, you've got to wonder **why** that fruit consistently flows from your root. It may reveal that there's some severe hurt or unresolved bitterness that needs to be resolved in yourself.

As you make the conscious decision to speak well of your spouse, it serves as a positive reinforcement. It's as if you're sowing the seeds that'll lead to the harvest you want more of. Consider these motivating forms of communication:

- Decide as a team to dig for gold. Honor what you admire about your spouse. As you discover unique traits, share it with them. Research has shown that as you speak well of others, it simultaneously reflects well on you. It's called spontaneous trait transference, where the traits you describe in others are attributed to yourself. Genuine words of affirmation, digging for and calling out positive features in your spouse, make you look good in their eyes.
- Develop a culture of calling out the good in the best way for your spouse to receive it. As you consistently play the game, you'll become a safe place for your partner. You'll establish an environment of trust. How would you feel if these sentences

were said to you: "I appreciate it when you do...," "I love it when you...," "You're an amazing mom/dad," "You really make people smile when you...," "Your words mean so much to the kids...," "I trust you...," "You're my safe place...," "I'm proud to call myself your wife/husband."

• Don't catastrophize in the heat of the moment.

If your spouse is singing the same song, and there's something that you don't agree with, or you know it doesn't fit your family's culture, be careful not to assume the worst of them. Remember, they are not your enemy and mean to do you no harm. Practice the power of the pause. They may be reacting out of habit or transition and need to be gracefully reminded of the gold in them. Instead of you responding off of their reaction, pause, and choose your words carefully.

This is not a race, but a day-to-day process of affirmations and encouragements. It takes a while to get a song out of your head and replace it with another. As long as you work together, you will get through this current season.

CHAPTER TAKEAWAYS

1. What has been the tone of your conversation lately? Do your words help or hurt?

2. Knowing that you only see an aspect of your spouse— caused by previous hurt or stress—what do you know is true about them? Can you call out the gold in them?

3. If you're the one who's changing, can you see and call out the gold in yourself?

5

Start from Where You Are

"It takes guts to stay married ... There will be many
crises between the wedding day and the golden
anniversary, and the people who make it are heroes."

—HOWARD WHITMAN

AROUND 1997, APPLE WAS ON THE VERGE OF A FINANCIAL CRI-
sis. Steve Jobs renewed his leadership efforts with the company and
brought it back to profitability in 1998. Apple then released the all-in-
one iMac, but they shocked the world when they removed the floppy
disc drive and introduced the world to USB. Good times man, good
times. The rest, as they say, is history. Currently, their stock prices are
through the roof, and the company is a force to be reckoned with.

Now I know my PC lovers are struggling with this chapter
already. So, I'll get to the point. What was the secret sauce of their
success? They're at the forefront of innovation, style, and quality.
Almost everything from iPods, iPhones, or iPads turn to gold. But
Apple would've never made it had they allowed their difficult circumstances to determine their worth. They had to persevere and

reinvent themselves. Steve Job said, "Sometimes when you innovate, you make mistakes. It is best to admit them quickly and get on with improving your other innovations."

As with Apple and many other companies that faced setbacks in their story, you must be willing to rebrand yourselves. Couples who quickly realize the ways of the good ol' days are no longer working, can innovate. Find new ways of making life work. Since they can't go back for a do-over, they start right from where they are. The sooner you learn from mistakes made, the faster you can improve upon the past to forge a new and better way.

Instead of being overwhelmed with the weight of financial losses, a family crisis, or dysfunctional behaviors, choose to move forward. Having learned lessons through the many ways things haven't worked, you can create, or, in some cases, rebuild the life you desire to live.

One writer on coping with change says that, "Change comes in many forms, but leaving behind what we know and are used to is almost always stressful, even if we've made the change ourselves."[7]

While navigating seasons of change, coping strategies are generally expressed into two categories: "escape" and "control." We may use a combination of both to cope in changing times. But leaning toward control strategies is a healthier way to work through challenges. The goal while going through difficulty is to regain self-control as you react through the four main stages of change, which are:

1. Shock and disorientation.
2. Anger with other emotional responses.
3. Coming to terms with the "new normal."
4. Acceptance and moving forward.

---

7. The Mind Tools Content Team by the Mind Tools Content Team et al., "Coping with Change. Facing Fear and the "New Normal." https://www.mindtools.com/pages/article/coping-with-change.htm.

The process of moving through these stages successfully depends on your ability to acknowledge your feelings, face the facts, remain hopeful, and give time to adapt."

I'm always amazed by the resilience of people who've lived through tornados. As they stand in ruins left behind in the wake of destructive winds, many are in shock. Though grateful to have survived, shock subsides, and soon they realize they're living in a nightmare. What do you do when your home is ripped to shreds by the unpredictable? As the camera crews interview residents of towns, you see the shock and bewilderment in the wake of the devastation. But then as they fight back the tears, they commit to rebuilding on the foundation of their ruins. To my surprise, they then turn and begin to go through the rubble, picking up treasure in what others see as trash—cleaning up the wreckage as they commit to rebuilding. People may ask, "Why not just pack it up and walk away? Just give up and quit." They respond, "It's my home. I'm not giving up. We will rebuild."

Root Yourself in This Moment

Are you in the process of beginning again? I, Sean, know all about starting over having moved to 17 different homes between the ages of 5 and 18. After a while, moving to a new place for me didn't seem like a big deal. In fact, I'm invigorated by conquering new places. Fast forward to my parenting years. While our children were in elementary school, we needed to move in order to keep them in a preferred school district. But our children struggled as we packed up in preparation to lease a new home. What blew my mind was the fact that the new residence was a few blocks down the road within the same neighborhood. I now understand that even if you're moving a block away, the moment you decide to relocate, you're beginning again. Whether being promoted on the job or changing careers altogether, you're in a phase of starting over.

There's a toll that transition takes on the soul. Although the promotion comes with higher pay, this new role is not your norm. Sure, the check is larger, but so are the consequences that accompany a new level of decision making. Add to that all the pressures of learning your new role while managing people who may have been passed up for your position. Without giving yourself time to process what's happening both personally and corporately, success may boomerang into future burnout. It may cause feelings of inadequacy or discontentment.

For instance, a couple has invested twenty-two long, and, yet, fulfilling years raising their child. It's time for the kids to venture out into the world and move out of the house. One spouse is left wondering why the other isn't leaping for joy. It's good news. We've successfully raised a child, now let's run around the house naked!

Meanwhile, the other spouse must process the grief of transitioning from their nurturing role to...well, what now? What fills the void now that the kids are out of the nest? Who are you now that the daily routine, the high school events, and people in the house are now gone? When you've prepared Sunday dinner as a feast for five and realize there was only a need to cook for two, grief can creep in. In some cases, couples struggle so greatly with children aging out of the house they may experience empty nest syndrome. Where parents are overcome with feelings of loneliness and grief after their kids depart from the home.

Couples in this season need to settle new roots within their new reality. Embracing the challenge of discovering new hobbies and enjoyable habits as a result of their newly found freedom. Ask yourselves what projects need to be pulled off the shelf? Are there any dreams I've put on hold while I raised my children? Could this be the perfect timing to bring delayed dreams into destiny? Should we downsize from our five-bedroom home and settle down in a more relaxing part of the city? Consider the consistency rate needed to establish a sense of connection via FaceTime or Zoom with your children to help you cope with this transition?

We've accepted the revelation that even good change is a great challenge to our emotional state of well-being. Imagine then how difficult the road ahead is in the aftermath of a marriage crisis. And many changes require starting over. If you want to break free from the futility of cycling through dysfunctional patterns of thought and counterintuitive behavior, welcome to the club! We're all about living a life filled with growth and productivity. So, in this chapter, we'll share introspective questions to answer, should you find yourself beginning again. Don't breeze through these questions of reflection. In doing so, you'll miss world-shaping truths that are only discovered through a critical and rigorous process.

Question number one: Why is our relationship valuable?

The meaning matters much more than we may realize. If you're not invested in the plot behind your own story, why would you fight to reach the end of the movie with passionate anticipation? We've discovered that couples who fail to grasp the significance of their marriage covenant are more susceptible to entertain the idea that starting over might not be worth it.

If you've been hurt, it's hard to hone in on why you should stay the course, especially as the glaring less-than-attractive problems of your partner and marriage ruminate in your mind. But press through the severe problems and strive to find the reasons why your marriage matters.

If I were to ask you, "Why should you stay together?" Could you articulate the good that will come as a result of your relationship? It must be more than the benefits, combined income, or staying the course for the sake of the kids until they move out of the house.

Another way to arrive at discovering your collective value is to discuss what has happened as a result of your relationship. What good has come about in the world through you? If you really can't land on a sufficient conclusion, try answering this question, "What value would you like to add to the world as a team?" There is a purpose to your marriage, and you have to seek it out. One of the best things we've ever done was to write our own obituary. That's right, we laid in the casket and imagined our close family members surrounded by friends and community. We listened as they reflected on the life we lived and the legacy we left behind. How did our marriage reflect the love of God to a broken world? Then we walked backwards and asked ourselves, "What must we do to become the kind of people who brought such meaning to the world?" Well defined purpose translates to determination and power.

This second question should be answered as soon as possible: Who will we turn to for help?

Here's the thing, both your friends and family carry a sense of bias. It may not be best to turn to those closest to you. Think about it. They know you. They've also heard, most likely from you, insider information. Objective support for your relationship's direction might not be a realistic possibility from your most intimate circle.

Overcoming painful experiences or opportunities for better, isn't easy. It would be best if you had wise counsel. If you're keeping confidentiality between one another, you're limiting the source of your support. Difficult discussions are filtered through the very individuals undergoing the challenge. It's like giving open heart surgery to yourself. It won't work.

The opposite extreme is that someone in the relationship is unwilling to go to anyone for fear of people "knowing their business." It's the ultimate trap against real transformation. It's similar to the prideful person who's exhibiting symptoms of apparent sickness but refuses to get a checkup from the doctor. Why won't they go? In their mind, "It'll all work itself out," or they act as if "When the doctor diagnosis it, then it becomes real." But it's real regardless of whether you go or not. And your spouse will tell you—if you listen—that it's not working itself out. It's getting worse. Should you land at a place where your partner refuses to get counseling, then *you* go. Take it upon yourself to seek the help you need during this time so that your heart can heal. Don't wait for your mate to get healthy.

My friend, please, if you get nothing else from this book, get wise, unbiased, professional help, and get it often. A wise, outside perspective offers you protection. "Well I've had a bad experience with counseling in the past..." Then solve that problem by finding a better fit, not by opting out of counseling.

Turning to others for help also prevents you both from fixing one another. You are not called to be their therapist. We have to get rid of the negative stigmas that exist around therapy. If you're a Christian, your pastor may be a great person, but not a professional therapist. Sure, you have an active relationship with Jesus, and you think that's enough for you. With all sincerity, you need **both** Jesus and therapy. God, throughout the Bible, worked miracles, counseled kings, and changed the world through people. Just as demonstrated in the Bible, He still works through professional people to help His children.

Marriage mentors are another level of connectedness that couples need. For years we've learned from our marriage mentors. Man, they've advised us through really tough moments. I remember a time when Sean was stuck and was wrestling with a major decision. No matter how hard I tried, I couldn't get him to open up to me. So, I texted our mentors. I told them what was going on, and one hour later, Sean's phone rang. I don't know what they shared, but Sean's tension subsided, and he snapped back to normal. I realized then that it didn't matter how hard I tried to share the truth, sometimes my husband needs a man in his life that can speak into him.

Find a couple through a small group in your church that you can turn to for advice. Take them out to dinner and receive. What's the harm in receiving wise help? The Bible tells us in Proverbs 11:14,

"Without good direction, people lose their way; the more wise counsel you follow, the better your chances" (MSG).

Who doesn't want better chances for success? When you're starting over, or if you need a do-over, don't lose your way. Get directions for your destination. God gives us wise couples as a personal GPS. Why fight to figure out the hard way what other people have suffered from learning? Humble yourselves and discuss deciding who you will turn to for help.

The third question to consider while starting from where you are is: What are our needs now?

Sometimes the 'same ol' date night places don't hit the spot anymore. In the previous seasons of your life, maybe the typical dating routine was sufficient, but things are different because, well, you've evolved. The stress levels or work-load on your job may have intensified. Shift changes and daily demands have hindered your quality time. One of you may be craving conversations that count as opposed to casual chats in passing. You have grown to a new level, and your needs have evolved. The thing is, you both may not be aware of it. An internal dissatisfaction grows within, nonetheless. Pinpointing why you're growing distant may be difficult without outside counsel.

You may desperately need to start your romantic life over from where you are now. If not, you'll remain stuck in a relational rut. Eventually, it will cause a deterioration of intimacy. After a while, you'll live as roommates rather than passionate lovers. Ultimately, you would end up managing kids and the bills minus the joy of having a fun and sexy partner in marriage.

Ask yourselves, "In this season of our lives, what are our needs now?" What is your hope, sexually? Describe your dreams for dating your mate. How can you recalibrate to help one another accomplish shared goals? When you have open communication with questions like these, you get clarity. Applying that clarity, you can come up with new plans that put you in a position to prosper now.

The key to unlocking the next level is in this question: What have we learned from the past?

Some people say, "Experience is the best teacher," but we believe ***learned*** experience is the best teacher. You've heard the old expression, "Hindsight is 20/20." And often, our mistakes make the road we should've taken clearer. But instead of kicking yourselves for stupid tax, maximize the gift of hindsight. Take advantage of the adversity. Learn from your shameful mistakes and even your bravest moments.

What have you learned in previous experiences? Does your wife get frustrated when you don't respond to her text? How can you adjust to address this if it's a reoccurring issue? If he hates it when you side-seat drive, can you leave that behavior in the rearview? Instead of going in circles, use the gift of knowing the nuances and rhythm of your past. Get ahead of the game when it comes to figuring out how to serve them. What do you know about one another now that you've arrived where you are?

This is one of the most powerful questions you can answer. Learning from the past breaks the pattern of harmful behaviors in the future. Let's say you've agreed on getting out of debt. Putting your heads together to create a solid plan that will change your family's financial line...but your favorite Friday night habit is to catch a movie at a theater connected to the mall. You've assessed your habits and discovered that leisurely strolls through the mall mean more than window shopping. It leads to spending real money. Money that you don't have available in the budget to spend. In this case, an honest assessment of the destructive patterns protects you in the present and preserves your hopes for a better future. So, you adjust where you enjoy date nights or choose to leave the debit cards at home to use the allocated cash you set aside for a night on the town.

To overcome dysfunctional habits, try to find the common denominator that keeps the hamster on the wheel. Learn to take a few steps back, pray, and assess similarities within your weaknesses.

Are there lessons that are screaming loud and clear that we continue to ignore?

Put your foot down and say we refuse to repeat the past! Now that we've exposed the truth, we'll be changed by it. We refuse to be married for the next ten years and still be immature in this area. Couples who want to outgrow where they've always been develop a habit of acknowledging the truth of who they are now and make the necessary changes to get them to where they want to be.

It's ok to recognize when it's time to get to know one another all over again. To fall in love with the person your spouse is currently, rather than who he or she used to be.

At this stage in the Reed marriage, we're walking up the edge of the hill. Hitting the tip of the midlife and honestly, we feel more influential than ever. It's a season of leading our kids as they transition from late teens into their early twenties. Our forties are full of slow metabolisms, an increase of gray hairs, hot flashes, and mentoring, simultaneously. After clashing with our adult children, we realized it was time to relinquish some responsibilities. They've arrived at a place where we're needed less as domineering caregivers and more as legacy leaders. We had to let go of the role we'd known for twenty years and lay hold to a new version of ourselves. And no, that was not an easy decision for me, Lanette. Family is a tremendous value, so naturally, we want the family together all the time. But that's not how life works, and honestly, the kids would go crazy. So, I weened myself off of them. As they grew older into their teens, I backed off trying to force family night, **every** night. I encouraged them to be free while Sean and I bumped up our dating and travel. After taking the time to process our new routine, we determined that our goal was that future generations would see in us what an intimate, Christ-centered love looks like.

The pressure is on for us to continue to model a passionate marriage. We're trying to age like fine wine. But for the first time since we married, we'll be empty nesters. It's been a long time since it's just been the two of us. Who are we without high school games, college move-in days, and an empty house? I guess we'll soon find out. Our mentors have all said they love it! Even though we don't know all that lies ahead, we're making plans to travel and see the world. Our budget is built to fund the exploration of new places. Even going so far as to fully fund annual family trips in different cities each year for our children and future grandchildren.

We're not sitting back passively, allowing life to happen to us. We refuse to be swallowed up in marriage boredom. Intentionality is the key. Being brave enough to reinvent and rebrand who we are in terms of our age and stage of life.

Listen, we've all made mistakes, but that's just part of life. The question is, what are you going to do with these lessons learned? Get proactive in nudging forward from point A to point Z. Remember, small steps still move you forward. Famed Canadian author L.M. Montgomery shared an amazing thought when she said, "Isn't it nice to think that tomorrow is a new day with no mistakes in it yet?"

In the next section of the book, we'll share how to fight with your spouse. But we're talking about picking the fights worth fighting for.

CHAPTER TAKEAWAYS

1. We read that learned experiences are the best teachers. So, choose a transition to focus on, what have you learned?

2. Are you repeating behaviors or moving forward from your learned experiences?

3. Would you consider having a mediator or seeing a marriage counselor to better your relationship? Why or why not?

COUPLES FIGHTS WORTH FIGHTING

6

Fight to Surrender

*"The idea of submission is never meant to allow
someone to overstep another's boundaries. Submission
only has meaning in the context of boundaries,
for boundaries promote self-control and freedom.
If a wife is not free and in control of herself, she is
not submitting anyway. She is a slave subject to a
slave driver, and she is out of the will of God."*

—HENRY CLOUD, BOUNDARIES IN MARRIAGE

TRANSITIONS SHOULDN'T ALWAYS BE PERCEIVED AS A NEGA-
tive thing. We must learn to look for the proverbial "silver lining" in
every situation. And you grow in age, you should increase in wisdom as you learn from life experiences. As you begin to process your
promotions, you must quickly adjust to new levels of blessings that
accompany your next season. One family, in particular, almost lost
their home because they were so overwhelmed with the responsibilities of life. Problems weren't the source of their tension, instead it was
the abundance of blessings.

In just a few years, they had four children. During their last child, the wife faced extreme pregnancy complications and was consistently hospitalized. The husband's role shifted from happy-go-lucky husband to on-call caregiver and daddy daycare. Add to that their two full-time jobs *with* promotions. All the while, maintaining heavy involvement in their church, paying off their two cars, moving into a newly built home, and caring for the needs of extended family members.

The weight of all of the responsibilities from each transition was so great that the husband began looking for an outlet to alleviate some of the pressure. In doing so, however, he began to neglect his responsibilities. Gradually, they stopped working as a team and began living as roommates. After burning both ends of the candlestick, he just wanted to give up. To break away from the stress, he would spend hours at a time playing video games as a mental escape. He just felt like he needed to conquer and win at something.

Although they made enough money, somehow, they were always behind paying the bills. There were holes in their pockets and things just didn't add up. Later on, he admitted that he would splurge on random purchases. Buying random electronics and household items, all the while knowing that the money wasn't there. This puts them in a deeper hole.

His wife was unaware of what was taking place in the finances because she was busy caring for their children, older family members, and working a full-time job. So, she delegated the funds to her husband. However, she never realized the real state of their finances. She would ask him if she could spend money on things they needed or something she wanted, and he would say yes even though the money wasn't there. He didn't want her to worry.

When we asked her why she didn't approach him earlier, she said, "I avoided the tough conversations about our finances because I didn't like the tension."

They were in a bad cycle. He would get frustrated, trying to explain what was going on. Both experienced a lack of sleep, junk-food-binge-eating, and resentment settled in.

She realized how far things had gone when she received a letter from the bank stating their home was about to be foreclosed for lack of payments. She finally had to stop running from the conversation and reached out to us for help. They needed wisdom, accountability, and an opportunity to catch up to what life had transpired, mentally.

For them, they decided that transparency was the only way they could overcome this transition. They chose to surrender to wise counsel to one another, and now the strength of their relationship can bear the load of their blessings.

In 1975, Muhammad Ali faced off against Joe Frazier. This was the third fight between two legendary fighters. This epic final battle is now known as "The Thrilla in Manila." After a brutal fourteen round battle, Joe's trainer, Eddie Futch, chose to throw in the towel as Ali gained the upper hand in the fight. Frazier's will was so strong that he wouldn't have quit. Despite the beating he was taking in the ring, and all the punishment he dished out on Ali, he refused to give up in his mind. His corner had to step in and make the call. Having counted the cost, they realized the battle for his life was more important than the fight in the ring.

After fighting in temperatures reaching 107 degrees, both Frazier and Ali took a beating that took a long-term toll. Neither fighter would ever fight the same. A part of themselves was poured out in the ring that day. Ali collapsed in the ring after seeing Fraziers' gloves come off. Later on, in an interview with swollen eyes and suffering exhaustion Ali said, "It was like death. Closest thing to dyin' that I know of." On the one hand, Ali won the match. On the other, both men gave so much of themselves to this violent contest; they may have lost more than they could've gained with a championship belt.

Is your fight to be right worth the prize you pursue? After all the effort placed in rounds against your partner, will the energy expended result in a glory that fades? Will intense debates, oppositional attitudes, and fighting in the ring result in any real winner? You see, there are fights worth fighting, and then there are battles where your will's resilience is remarkable. But after you've won, there's more damage done than good. I'm suggesting you throw in the towel in the bouts against your spouse. That's right, wave the white flag and give up to escape further punishment in a losing battle. There's a safer and more successful way to win the struggles you're in as a team. Let's dive into the fight to surrender to your spouse.

What in the World Does it Mean to Surrender in Marriage?

The root of the word surrender is "to give something up," or "to give oneself up." It's a commitment to give yourself **entirely** to your spouse. To be all in, meaning you're holding nothing back. You are devoted to a life of complete vulnerability towards each other. It's putting one another first and looking out for each other. Myles Munroe said, "Submission is the willingness to give up our right to ourselves, to freely surrender our insistence on having our own way all the time."

Throwing in the towel may initially sound like a cop-out. Surrendering may appear as cowardice at first glance. But as you chew on the definition of surrender, you'll soon come to grips with just how scary yielding truly is. It's creating an invitation for an invasion. After you've mustered up the courage to share your needs and desires, your spouse may tune you out while scrolling through Facebook as you spill your guts. What if they reject you when you try to open up? Surrendering in marriage is a fight against the fears and anxiety within yourself as you brace for the unknown. You are opening your heart to someone with a high possibility of being misunderstood. Will your spouse accept you, retaliate against you, or stand with you in full support? It takes bravery to be naked and not ashamed before your spouse.

Some people see this as a weakness, while others realize it's a strength. We've come from different backgrounds and family dynamics that shape our perspectives. Either way you see it, and regardless of where you've come from, your partnership's potential is unlocked as you're fighting on the same team in the ring for authenticity and acceptance. The key to a dream marriage is found in opening your mate's heart. One of your highest callings in marriage is to help your spouse become who God made them to be. How can you do this when you're only focused on yourself or if you've never honestly heard, valued, and understood who they were?

Surrender Your Ears

"Lend me your ears! Listen to me and understand." That's the cry of an unheard spouse. *The person who surrenders their ears actively, listens to understand correctly.* "Did I hear you say that, right? What did you mean when you said...?" Choose to give yourself to them in the moment. Be there in the room with them rather than your so-called followers out there on social media. While they speak, your email notifications are a distraction from your dream marriage. Make eye contact with them as they share their heart with you. What you may discover as you hear their hearts, you'll absorb insider information. Step by step, you'll gradually grow in intimacy as you give yourself to doing the little things you've gleaned as you've listened. You were able to receive it because you chose to be present. Cutting out the distractions from your most important priority. They can grow to a greater sense of security since you've shown them you care by fully being there.

A surrendered ear silently listens without interrupting what they're saying. I, Lanette, have a hard time doing this. And I have to make every effort to calm myself down and listen so that I can fully understand what Sean's saying. It's not my heart to interrupt and dis-regard what he says, but that's what my actions communicate by cut-ting him off. Don't listen to respond, hear them to receive. The fight to surrender is a battle within yourself for maturity. A mindset that says it's not about being right or proving them wrong. It's humility that hon-ors your spouse's heart. They have something to say, and it matters. I'm open to their perspective, even though I may disagree with what they have to say. I choose to suck it up and listen up. I am resisting the need to be right while accepting their need to be heard. In fact, you're fully aware that you just might learn something new. Proverbs 18:13 says, *"Spouting off before listening to the facts is both shameful and foolish."*

Then, as you prepare to share, don't 'one up' them in the con-versation. Take a moment to acknowledge what you've heard from them. Resist the urge to rush to judgment. Ask a question in support of what they've shared like, "I didn't know you felt that way—how can I do better next time?" Or "What can I adjust to support you in this area?" Process their transparency before you trample over them. It's not about winning against them. It's about winning as a couple. Ask clarifying questions and even take a break if you're beginning to take things personally. Create a flow where you can share your heart and be heard as well. Try to ask questions that facilitate open feedback rather than falling into the trap of giving one-word answers.

Surrender Your Hands

I once had a soon-to-be wife request that I replace the word *submit* within the traditional marriage vows. She found the very idea of the term somewhat repulsive. I shared with her that from God's point of view, submission isn't a derogatory ideal. It was never intended to imply a life of living as a doormat for an abusive spouse. Conceptually, submission has a bad rap from false manipulators, womanizers, and false teachers who perpetuate subservient ideals over women.

But Scripture actually instructs both men and women to submit in Ephesians 5:21:

"Submit to one another out of reverence for Christ" (NIV).

The root word comes from "Sub" meaning to come under, and *mittere* which means to send on a mission. The idea is to yield your mission to someone else's consideration. As a surrendered husband begins to make plans for the home, he realizes it's "our home" and yields to include his wife's wisdom. Wives with strong wills and leadership skills pause their plans to hear from their man. Submission and surrender are synonymous.

Scripture teaches us that Jesus chose to serve people in Matthew 20:28:

"For even the Son of Man came not to be served but to serve others and to give his life as a ransom for many."

More specifically, He served broken people. He sacrificed himself to unify the family. Out of reverence for our Lord, we follow His example of becoming the ultimate servant in our homes, finding ways to yield your will to serve their needs, and sometimes even their wants. When you both operate in this mindset, it becomes a competition to out-bless one another.

Our selfish nature is thinking, "What about me and my needs? Or, "What if I already contribute more to the marriage?" I'm going to challenge you to shift your focus. Instead of seeking to be served, discover the joy of serving. Haven't you heard, it's more blessed to give than to receive?

Be willing to invest in their interest. As you study their passions, you understand the pathways to their heart. Schedule date nights around their favorite hobbies, even if you're not passionate about the activity. When you've transitioned from focusing on yourself to serving someone else, aiming to please them is a way of honoring them. Just as Christ served, you sacrificially serve your spouse willingly.

I, Sean, am a semi-pro baker. My recipes are "state famous." Not quite world famous yet. When I bake cookies, there's only so many that can fit on the baking sheet per batch. As I remove the first round of chocolate chip goodness, my family clamors to pick the best looking among the bunch. What they also tend to do is look for an equal amount of portions. It's all about fair servings. If it's not entirely identical, a war breaks out.

Let's keep it real; we want fair reciprocity. If I scratch your back, I'm looking for you to scratch mine. And you better do it just as well as I did it for you! From the moment we operate with this mentality, we lose the match. As your heart grows mature, you'll exchange an exhausting life of scorekeeping for the joy of generosity. No, it's not always easy, but it is rewarding to relinquish a life of record keeping. Instead of carrying the weight of their efforts, focus on the works of your own hands.

As we share the true meaning of surrender during marriage conferences, the question always arises, "Am I supposed to submit to my spouse when they're in the wrong? Are we expected to follow someone who's out of line?"

The answer is complex in that it's both no and yes. We're not in the least bit suggesting the abandonment of reason, blindly following a wayward partner into unhealthy actions or unwise decisions. In fact, true surrender or submission begins in the heart. It's a conscious decision to release control of your spouse's actions and reactions towards you.

You are choosing to honor who they are, even though you may disapprove of the perception. In your home, you have the power to say no when necessary. Couples have the right to disagree without filing for divorce. Choosing to live in harmony while holding widely different views and values is ok. It's saying, "I love you, but not so much the direction you're leading us in." Healthy couples who work with this mindset may hit a fork in the road, but not in their relationship. They'll pause, pray, listen, and then say what they feel—working together to reach a point of agreement on a course of action. Since they had the right mindset to begin with—a servant's heart surrendered to their spouse—they were never in jeopardy. Their choices may have been delayed, but their dreams aren't denied.

It boils down to an awareness of how power struggles are unfruitful. This takes us back to our strike-slip faults, normal faults, and thrust faults in chapter one. When left unchecked, couples become stalemates—stuck like strong-willed fighters in the ring—exhibiting behaviors like stonewalling or shutting down effective communication until they get what they want. Some use oppositional behaviors that keep their families stuck in offense and ultimately unproductive. Even if one spouse caves into the other, they feel manipulated in the process. They won't be happy on the journey to where they're headed.

But if you practice submission, it shows your spouse that you're committed to solving the problem by working together to find a solution. We may not see eye to eye on how to get there, but we do agree to respect one another along the way. The goal is to figure it out without fighting each other and refusing to make the decisions more critical than the deciders. Instead, we'll fight to surrender.

Recently, we decided to sell some furniture online. We disagreed with the sales prices. Lanette was going for a lower rate to move the items faster. In contrast, Sean was trying to get top dollar. Early on in our marriage, this was the perfect setup for an argument. But instead, we listened to one another and found a middle ground that sold everything we listed in one weekend.

A healthy couple says, "Here's where we are, there's where we want to go, and with you is where I want to be along the way." From that emotionally aware and healthy place, they are on the same team.

They are determined to protect their oneness from any problem try-ing to pull them apart.

One thing that'll demotivate a spouse from following the other is poor leadership. More specifically, a bad attitude. No one wants to follow, let alone work with someone that wants to dish out com-mands. "Do this, do that, and get it done as soon as possible." If you're the spouse wishing to make it easier to receive your leadership, then empower them. Let them know that their voice adds value and that you see them as equally important to the direction of the decisions. "Honey, what do you think the best course of action is?" Or, "I'd like to get your input so we can make the best choice."

Choosing to Collaborate Over Control

As you join forces, your power is multiplied against problems. Collaboration is defined as a joint effort to create something as a team. Marriage is the commingling of your mind, soul, and body. We believe that oppositional forces set up against marriage recog-nize the strength of numbers. Your power is multiplied exponen-tially when you agree to join hand in hand and develop your dreams. Working together requires control, but in this case, we're talking about *self-control*. Managing your temperament and conducting yourself in a mature manner is a prerequisite skill set for success. Too often, immature people get defensive because they feel they'll lose ground. This anxiety disrupts unity. Circling this mountain is counterproductive. Instead, choose to collaborate over fighting for control. We teach couples to schedule appointments to discuss everything: financial goals, sexual expectations, parenting decisions, and conversations for clarifying incidents, just to name a few.

Without a set time to hash out what's been pent-up within, you'll eventually feel as if your contribution to current events is weakened. This is when we start exhibiting unhealthy techniques to gain ground.

Insecurity, arrogance, pride, or fear jump in the driver's seat, and our behavior begins to go 100 miles an hour in the wrong direction.

If you're beginning to put your guard up, maybe your ego is wounded. There's a signal being sent from your spouse that you're interpreting as a threat. Take your foot off of the gas and remember to breathe. Find your way back to the reality that your spouse is **not** your enemy.

Before you react to the movie playing in your mind, schedule a time to clarify what they meant. It's worth the extra effort to make time to understand. Take a step back and gather yourself before jumping to conclusions. Be determined to end the drama before it begins by checking yourself before checking *them*.

Is it possible that they've behaved in a manner that reminds you of who they once were? Could it be that your perspective is tying them from this present moment to a past event? Adjust your preconceived notions of what you assume about them. Remember this: assumptions lead to dysfunction. Living as mind readers rather than listeners is a recipe for disaster, whereas honor makes room to see all sides of the issues at hand. It says, "I love you enough to listen and learn." Well-rounded relationships grow through leaders who broaden their understanding through healthy communication. Solution-oriented people ask questions like, "What do you mean when you say this?" Rather than creating their own conclusion that may lead to condemnation and separation.

I Still Don't Know If I'm Comfortable with the Idea of Surrender

Maybe you're still on the fence with the concept of submission. It may conjure up feelings of weakness, defeat, or forfeiture, and it doesn't sound like something you want to get in the habit of trying. But from the moment you started dating, you began to practice the art of surrender. Anytime you give yourself for the benefit of others, you exchange your power for their good. You can't truly love without yielding some of your wants to meet their needs.

Did you know that the opposite of love isn't hatred? It's actually fear. But a culture of love drives out fear. Love creates an atmosphere of acceptance for who you are. This provides security as a result of knowing that a person won't abandon you when you fail. You know that they're not into you for what you do, but honestly, for the person God created you to be. True love builds a bridge of trust that's held up by mutual respect. **Trust** assures your spouse, "I'm not here to hurt you. I believe that we're here to help one another." **Mutual respect** says, "I know that you can contribute no matter what the cause." Surrender thrives in a trust-filled environment, and trust grows in an atmosphere of love.

You see, love is a verb. So, actions and reactions must demonstratively facilitate a safe space that's rejection free. But fear kicks in if an attitude of superiority is shown. When dominance drives one or both individuals, fear and pride will block intimacy.

When the culture you've created revolves around the need to be right and proving them wrong, it stunts your growth. So why continue to foster a toxic culture? You can do something to change this starting today. Fight the right fight to surrender rather than superiority.

As you practice this new culture, you intensify the weight of your words. Because you've led with love, vulnerability, and humility, you've cast aside hostility and angst. Since their unhealthy actions or misguided emotions don't rule you, you're not a victim. You're in control and creating a new culture of communication and negotiation.

Submission in no way means passively going along for the ride. It's knowing what to say, when to say it, what questions to ask, and how to work together to forge the future you've always dreamed about. Think of it as dancing. While getting your grove on, you can sense the shifts needed to maintain rhythm. As you glide, you give leeway for your spouse to take the lead, and in turn, they do the same as you strut your stuff on the dance floor.

> 1 Peter 3:7 says, *"In the same way, you husbands must give honor to your wives. Treat your wife with understanding as you live together. She may be weaker than you are, but she is your equal partner in God's gift of new life. Treat her as you should so your prayers will not be hindered."*

Honor is a gift that must be given away to exist. When it's not actively shared with your spouse, in some way, you dishonor them. In these verses, it says to give her understanding and treat her as an equal partner. Here is God's idea of a successful husband. The weaker vessel part refers to our physical differences and is in no way an insult to women. He's saying to men that although you're physically stronger, don't allow your emotional side, attitude, or actions to treat her in an oppressive manner. She should in no way be made to feel subservient. If she's going to follow you, it will be if she decides, not due to an overpowering imposition. If you find yourself turning to any one or more of these tendencies, it's counterproductive. Stop doing it immediately and switch to a new and loving way of servant-leadership. I know this hit hard for some guys out there. This is a stretch for you, and it's an area of needed growth. Start from where you are, but *start,* nonetheless. Little by little, you'll repair the ripples of your relationship. Trust will be restored as she finds a safe place in your graciousness towards her. Check out 1 Peter 3:4-6,

> *"The same goes for you wives: Be good wives to your husbands, responsive to their needs. There are husbands who, indifferent as they are to any words about God, will be captivated by your life of holy beauty. What matters is not your outer appearance— the styling of your hair, the jewelry you wear, the cut of your*

clothes—but your inner disposition. Cultivate inner beauty, the gentle, gracious kind that God delights in. The holy women of old were beautiful before God that way, and were good, loyal wives to their husbands. Sarah, for instance, taking care of Abraham, would address him as "my dear husband." You'll be true daughters of Sarah if you do the same, unanxious and unintimidated" (MSG).

Make a note, ladies, that your tone sets the mood. The best way to achieve the most fruitful results is to consider your approach. I'm not suggesting walking on eggshells, just check your demeanor and your delivery. You have the pleasure of setting the thermostat of the home through your attitude. So, adjust it intentionally. Passive men tend to frustrate goal-oriented women. Not in every case, but many well-meaning ladies up the pressure to prompt some semblance of a pulse. Yet this approach may push him further into a shell as he loses a wife and starts feeling like he's being mothered. Simply stated, humility helps him hear your heart. Men are more defensive when they feel attacked, overly criticized, or nagged. There's a beauty beyond your body that catches his eye, and that, ladies, is a surrendered heart. Colossians 4:6 says, *"Let your conversation be gracious and attractive so that you will have the right response for everyone."*

Maybe the issue is we never transitioned into a servant's role even though it was required from the moment we said, "I do". We read the covenant but missed the fine print for the product called marriage to work. But the manufacturers manual, in this case, The Bible, totally lays out how essential mutual submission is to success.

During transitions, it's imperative we create this culture to preserve unity. That is tough if you were never taught. It's difficult to swallow, especially if you're resistant due to a previous harmful relationship. Walls of defensiveness surrounding a wounded soul must come down so the wounded soul can be made whole. The past must be mended for your present relationship to move forward.

At some point, you must trust one another. The only way to ignite trust is to entrust into their care things you care about. They may not get it all right, so give grace, but grow together.

CHAPTER TAKEAWAYS

1. Based on the definition we provided for submission, do you have a difficult time submitting?

2. Why do you think you have a difficult time? Try to be as clear as possible.

3. We focused on choosing to collaborate over fighting for control. If you have a hard time submitting or controlling, when can you collaborate to create unity rather than division?

7

Fight for Closeness

"The single biggest problem in communication
is the illusion that it has taken place."

—GEORGE BERNARD SHAW

IN 2019, INSIDER.COM CONDUCTED A STUDY WITH PEOPLE who had previously been married and were about to get married again. Seventy-five percent of the people surveyed said a lack of commitment played a part in the demise of their marriage.[8] Feeling alone in your own home is a sad reality for many people who've drifted away from one another. This is why you must win in the fight for closeness.

Confidence shoots through the roof when you're assured of the fact that your spouse has your back. As life throws unexpected blows of unimaginable pain, your partner should be your safe place. Your family legacy and dreams are contingent on working together on the same team. If you endeavor to work together, you'll have to sharpen your skills, starting with how to have effective conversations.

8. Gabbi Shaw, "These Are the 11 Most Common Reasons People Get Divorced, Ranked." (Insider, January 31, 2019). https://www.insider.com/why-people-get-divorced-2019-1.

The fight for closeness is won by couples committed to vulnerable communication. Opening lines of introspective conversation can lead to successful collaboration. Should you feel the tremors of transition, try some of these suggestions together.

TIP #1: Set Your Mindset

Before diving into in-depth discussions, develop the right mindset. This is the kind of thinking that always keeps the end result in mind. Zoom way out into the future, what's the desired outcome? Take a moment to calculate what you really want. What will you accomplish by going through with the conversation? Is there a negotiation to be made? Are you open to learning from their perspective? What's going on in your spouse's mind? As best as you can imagine, see the conversation in advance. Try and view things from their perspective. How will this benefit the other person? Upon reflection, you'll gain confidence in knowing that your loving spouse desires growth for you both. So, although it'll be challenging, it's also rewarding.

Be mindful of the fact that you both have strengths as well as weaknesses. So even if you feel that they're at fault, it doesn't mean that they lack insight at that moment. An array of anxiety, fear, anger, and many other emotions arise at the thought of confrontation for some. It takes courage to confront your spouse, especially if you're second-guessing whether this will be a healthy confrontation.

Talk it out in your head first. This tip helped Lanette a lot. If you're timid or shy by nature, the right mindset is essential. Mustering up the courage to overcome the second-guessing in your head is key to sharing what's in your heart. If you believe thoughts like *The last time I tried to speak up, I failed*, or *I'm afraid that I won't be heard*, you'll never come out of your shell. What's worse is that you're being held hostage in a prison of your own emotions. Press through the hesitance with some much-needed self-talk. This may not go perfectly, but at least it'll be a step in the right direction.

Speak from your perspective. For example, instead of saying, "You don't care about me," try "When this happened, it made me feel like..." The moment we invoke the word "you" in a confrontational exchange, a defensive wall rises against the accusation. It's worth privately processing "I" statements rather than "you" statements.

Stick to one subject per discussion. You've done everything to get a captive audience. For some of you, for the first time in a long time, you've got their undivided attention. Resist the urge to release 50 discussions all at once. As the old saying goes, Rome wasn't built in a day, and every issue in your marriage won't be resolved in one conversation. Sticking to one subject at a time may prove to be more productive in that you're laser focused. The greater the bullseye, the more likely you'll hit the center point and solve the problem. Check your emotions before engaging in your chat. If you're angry, wounded or anxious, it may have less to do with them, and more to do with the movie replaying in your mind. I can't tell you how many times I was fuming about an offense that my wife didn't even realize she'd done. By the time we finished talking, it was a huge misunderstanding. We've learned to feel what we're feeling, examine the reasons why and schedule a time to address the issue. But it all goes out the window if you approach the meeting with untamed emotions.

TIP #2 Napkin the Need

It was a cold winter's day in 1998. As was our custom, Lanette and I sat down to chat at Denny's restaurant. It was a hangout spot, and we were addicted to the 'moon over my hammy' and buffalo chicken strips. This time was different, though. It's as if we'd awakened from a deep sleep of the soul. Realizing in that conversation, there was an absolute void of unfulfilled desires. At that moment, we pulled out a pen and began to write out on a napkin our internal needs and ways to meet them. We wrote our values and built a vision around them.

You can get as fancy as you want with this. Try writing your ideas on a whiteboard or brainstorming them in a shared Google document. We have a resource on our website that we created just for this. It's called "Our Blueprint." Whatever you use, take the time to get on the same page regarding your priorities. Get your wants and needs out in the open. The key to this exercise is to take turns listening while your spouse share's their ideas or feelings. Try your best while listening to take notes and hear what they're saying before giving a response. Then share your thoughts. As you share your priorities, you'll draw closer as you express your needs. Since they cannot read your mind, articulating *your* needs is *your* job. The napkin exercise can be both fun and focused, but the goal is that it's converted to actionable intel that you can build on.

One of the strengths of our marriage is that both of us carry the bottom-line organizer gene. We've been together long enough to know that we both bring value to the table. We lead with statements like, "What do you think about..." or "Do you have a sense of peace about this decision." But we'll never make a move until we agree on where we're going. To this day, we continue to napkin out our needs. The napkins have since been replaced with numbers on spreadsheets for budgets, vision-mapping whiteboards, and dinners filled with dreaming about our future legacy.

We truly respect the value of what we bring individually to the team. I'm the left eye, and Lanette's the right eye of our vision. When we equally see what we believe God is saying, we capture the full scope of vision. The moments of our greatest intense fellowships come when we dig a trench in the ground and hold tightly to our truth. When we fight to prove one another wrong, it often ends in a stalemate. Our most significant results came through the patient process of listening to learn. We increased the scope of our wisdom through *both-and*, rather than *either-or*. Considering both perspectives and building from the collective wisdom and contribution gained from both points of view.

TIP #3 Take a Timeout If Things Get Too Intense

Don't attempt to turn a large ship at sea with a sharp turn. Course correction must be done correctly. It took time for you to get to where you are, and this isn't a race to change. So, try to pace the conversation. Stop when you sense the ship is about to capsize. If the chat is growing contentious, manage first and foremost your own emotions. If criticisms about ideas turn into insults towards one another, you're not achieving—you're attacking. It's more destructive than constructive. An hour-long pause may be just what the doctor ordered to gather your composure. Take a jog around the block, eat a Snickers bar, pray a little bit, and breathe. Now that you've calmed down, come back to the conversation.

If you hit a wall while sharing your feelings, find a more direct way that cuts through the confusion. Try leading off with statements like, "What I need is free-time from watching the kids, and work. Once per week I'd like to have a day to get away and have *me time*." Rather than saying, "I feel overwhelmed," it helps when you give clear examples of what you need, rather than trying to figure out a resolution. From here, you can agree on a day off, allocate funds in the budget for the 'me time,' and work out childcare to meet the need for respite.

TIP #4 Schedule Appointments with Your Spouse

Need a doctor's appointment? Guess what you'll have to do? Call the doctor's office and schedule an appointment. Why? Your check-up requires a physician's undivided attention. Setting the time and place makes you the priority at that moment. The higher the priority, the more you're required to schedule appointments.

Set aside time to discuss your needs, wants, frustrations, or desires. The last thing you want to do is dump a deep conversation in a shallow attention span. Asking a guy how he feels while his eyes are glued to the game will never yield positive results. If she's half-asleep, but you want to discuss sexual dissatisfaction, prepare to be disappointed with the results.

The benefits are numerous, but here are a few significant reasons to implement this strategy as soon as possible. The first reason is the time created to clarify the foundation of the conversation. What's most exciting to you? Is there a specific action they can implement to better the family? How can you frame your words in a way that minimizes accusations and opens dialogue?

The second reason is that they can commit to speaking with undivided attention. In doing so, they also agree to the conversation. They become willing participants in the process. A bonus is that you can pray before you say what you need to say. You can release any toxic emotions that may derail your intended destination.

Determine how often you need to have conversations. Our frequency is once per week. It's not always confrontational either. It's time set aside to talk out what we're processing within. Remember, seventy-five percent of couples say that a significant contributing factor to their divorce was a lack of commitment to the marriage. There will always be a game, there's always a pile of clothes to wash, but your spouse is precious and should be given the attention they deserve. Setting time aside to hear your spouse's heart says, "I'm committed to you, and I value what you're feeling."

Making a habit of having meaningful conversation prevents toxic build-up. As misunderstandings marinate in the back of your mind, the lens over your heart gets morphed. When you address the background noise, you eliminate the static that's causing confusion and hindering closeness. Use these appointments to exchange grace and mercy instead of insults and condemnation. It isn't about shifting blame or blasting your spouse. To prevent a judgmental attitude and hurling accusations, you plan clarifying conversations.

TIP #5 Release Your Anticipated Reactions

If you walk into the conversation trying to force your desired response, it's unlikely that you'll get your desired results. Effective communication is rooted in understanding. It happens when both partners feel heard. All perspectives and positions should be shared. The opportunity for a fair hearing of opinions through open dialogue offers hope that maybe there's a compromise to be made. But when you both feel unheard, motivation falls flat, and so goes the purpose of the conversation. Even if you make progress and they agree to go along with your perspective, an internal resentment towards you may undermine your plan.

Silently listen without developing a reply. Some may find moments of vulnerability uncomfortable—processing and sharing emotions stir up an internal gag reflex. You'd rather people "get to the point and say it already." If you can relate, this point is crucial. Silently listening without developing a reply, applies to your body language as well. Shaking your head in disagreement rejects their perspective. A lack of control over fidgety limbs may send a signal of "I don't want to be here or hurry up and get to it." Don't force out of them what they're slowly processing with you. What you'll discover is that it's not always about you giving a solution to their problem. The comfort comes as you offer your undivided attention so they can be heard. As uncomfortable as it may be for those who see vulnerability as a weakness let your spouse feel what they're feeling. Give them space to cry or slowly express themselves without condemnation. Listen with open ears as they express themselves without interruption.

One of the definitions of vulnerability is to be capable of being wounded emotionally or physically. As people let down their defense to share their innermost thoughts intimately, they're more susceptible to being hurt. An atmosphere of trust is a must for transparency. Patrick Lencioni says, "Teamwork begins by building trust. And the only way to do that is to overcome our need for invulnerability." So, sarcasm, snide remarks, insulting their intelligence, or attacking their honesty may wound them. Belittling them, putting words in their mouth, or stirring up anger is ineffective. Don't respond with retaliation. You may want to say, "I didn't know you felt like that, how can I help." Or genuinely say, "I'm sorry that I hurt you."

The goal is to grow closer through conversation and even confrontation. When people hear the word confrontation, it carries a negative connotation. But the root of the word confront is "face." It's to stand face-to-face with your spouse with nothing hidden. Seeing that you love your spouse should go without saying. The goal of confrontation in marriage is to share your heart while humbly hearing theirs.

Forming a reply while someone is sharing is an excellent technique for debate, but not for relational development. That goes for your body language as well. If you're shaking your head "no" while they're speaking, it shuts what they're saying down—creating an atmosphere of contention rather than heartfelt conversation. Keep in mind that it's not about winning an argument. It's all about increasing intimacy, which takes place through vulnerability.

TIP #6 Become a Complimentary Couple

When was the last time you gave a genuine compliment? They need your admiration. Even when they're at their worst, they need your affirmation. If prepping for a conversation, jot down a few compliments as a couple, and share the compliments before getting into criticism. Try to find three to five positives to the one negative that you'll share. I know you might not feel like saying something nice when you're upset, but that's precisely why you should do it—to remind you of why you love them. That they're not all bad, and that you're not perfect! It humbles you, while simultaneously setting an atmosphere of grace for them. The goal here is to release tension by expressing the reasons why you love one another. A little praise for your partner goes a long way.

As you grow closer, you will discover so much about one another, including your marriage's purpose. As your communication increases and notices the gold in them, you'll awaken to find that there *is* a reason you two are together. It's bigger than just work, but the purpose of your marriage is waiting on the other side of unity.

CHAPTER TAKEAWAYS

1. Out of all of the suggestions listed in this chapter, which do you and your spouse actively implement?

2. Which areas do you need to work on?

3. How can you keep one another accountable?

8

Fight for Freedom

"Inherited beliefs are the trojan horses of our childhood."

—PAUL SCANLON

THIS FIGHT, QUITE POSSIBLY, MAY BE THE MOST SIGNIFICANT battle you'll face together. Whether you know it or not, there's an ongoing war over your shared identity—who you are as a team. Healthy couples thrive when they walk in freedom from past scars. They're free to dream their way forward. Having discovered why they are together, their imagination is unlocked. They are focused on shaping the world as a Kingdom-minded couple. Often contemplating who they'll leave a unique mark on in this world when they've fulfilled their purpose.

In answering the tough questions about identity, purpose, and self-actualization, you discover reasons to persevere. It's challenging to do so individually, let alone as a couple, but I assure you, it's worth the energy and effort. **Meaning** matters in the middle of marriage transitions. When couples forget about "their why," they lose the drive to press through difficult times. But if you get on the same page about your purpose together, you will conquer your problems because your legacy is on the line.

This is a huge point. There has never been another marriage like yours. No one has ever gone through the same transitions as you have. It is true that people's experiences are similar, but you're not exactly the same. Working through your unique experience is deeply personal and somewhat exploratory. When you come to grips with this, you understand the value of learning methods from other marriages, while also knowing that you must find your own meaning. It's great to look to others for helpful strategies, wisdom, and tips. By all means, find mentors, and glean as much as you can from them. After "eating the meat" of what others offer, spit out the bones of the things that don't fit you. From there, lean into the Lord and to one another to find your footing moving forward. Then, you can say with security and a sense of clarity, "this is us." Sadly, many in this world will never discover their purpose because they're distracted by problems. The thing is, some issues are present because you've yet to discover your purpose.

Early in our marriage, we fell in line with some of the protocols from our parents. Typically, they worked, came home, cooked food, and watched TV. And there's absolutely nothing wrong with that life—for them. After all, they earned that right. When we got married, we fell into the same custom, and within a few years, we ran into a problem with marriage boredom. We were glued to the television screen, being inundated with the noise of advertisements, sitcoms, and the nightly news. Consequently, we were missing out on our own story. We watched movies of couples exploring new places, while feeling trapped in the self-made prison of our apartment. Why? Because we didn't take the time to explore who we were, rather than where we came from. Now please hear me, we're grateful for our upbringing. This is not a knock against our roots. But family is a foundational root for you to grow your **own** branch and produce your own unique fruit.

The root of our marriage boredom was a lack of knowing who we were, which would've led us to activities that would bring us fulfillment. In short, we were wasting our time because we didn't know the meaning of our lives. After "napkining" the need, we found out that Lanette liked adventure, and I loved excitement. We took the lid off for a moment and dreamed as big as possible.

What did that look like practically? For Lanette, it was traveling somewhere she'd never been before. For Sean, it meant bungee jumping once we arrived at Lanette's destination. So that was our answer: make a bucket list of places to visit and research fun things to do upon arrival. It sounds nice, but we couldn't afford the level of our imagination yet, so we started from where we were. We began by visiting every museum we'd never been to in the city. It was free and most often was located near restaurants we'd never tried. Sean was excited to eat new food, and Lanette was out of the house exploring a new place!

Can you imagine how miserable we were while sitting there, wasting away on the couch? Now we know that part of our purpose as a marriage team is to travel the country sharing our story in marriage conferences. We've even traveled overseas and encouraged leaders in places that we'd dreamed of in a Denny's on a napkin decades before. At this point in our children's lives, they have traveled much more than we ever did by their ages. The same mindset of exploring the world and creating adventures runs in them. This is modeled in Jeremiah 29:11, *"For I know the plans I have for you," says the LORD. "They are plans for good and not for disaster, to give you a future and a hope."*

God had a plan for us that was bigger than being couch potatoes who watched stories on TV that they'd never live themselves. We were living contrary to our identity. On the surface, we were bored of one another. At the root, we weren't planted in our purpose. When we don't operate according to our Creator's unique design, we're dysfunctional. If we're dysfunctional, we'll be dissatisfied until we discover our dream.

We can all "dream" in the sense of imagining what we want our lives to become and marriages to achieve. Our hope is to stir up the passion within you to set your dreams on a course for reality. Over the next few chapters, we will show you how to receive God's plan for your marriage, create a shared vision, and agree on a purpose that will greatly benefit this world from concept to completion. We firmly believe that your vision or dream can be accomplished, but it won't come by accident. This requires determination and teamwork, but the work is worth it because accomplishing your goals is not only for your benefit. It is for future generations and all those who are within your sphere of influence as well.

Your Shared Vision *Is* Your Reality. So, Tell Me, What Do You See?

While writing a chapter in this book, I sat at a Starbucks. An older gentleman sat down across from me, and proceeded to talk about every problem in our nation: healthcare, government spending, corruption within bureaucracy, etc. The list continued on and on until finally I politely dismissed myself from the conversation. I don't think he meant anything harmful, but he was venting to the wrong brother.

It doesn't profit us to complain about the problems of our family, community, technology, educational systems, or society if we're not going to do anything about it to enhance it? Anyone can whine, but it takes guts to rise from ruins and transform a **complaint into a cause**. What are you, a complainer, or a cause-maker? Sometimes the very thing that irritates us the most is an indicator of our cause. It's the place of our purpose. This place is where you discover your dream.

We're in a time where people need world-enhancing visions that'll attempt great things. Forget about blaming others for the problems of the world, instead endeavor to correct them. Some couples have made drastic mistakes or are afraid to take chances. But becoming an agent of change requires risk-taking. Are you willing to find your dream that makes your marriage worth fighting for? Change for the better requires individuals to discover a shared dream. Now, what do we mean when we refer to *a dream*? A dream is a strongly desired goal or purpose. A great question to ask yourself is what problem can our lives become the solution to? Where does our passion meet a problem? The marketplace has a problem that our creativity can solve. Our community has a void that our talents can fill. A child has no home and we've got extra rooms. The educational system is struggling where our mentoring is strong. There's a church with members but very few mentors. You see the problem, but have you come to see your ability as the solution?

Some of you have yet to discover that dream because you fear embracing the enormity of what you see. Big dreams can be intimidating. You may look at your cause and its daunting. In part, because it's such a huge problem and from your perspective you can't solve it all. Or maybe you just don't know where to start. To this thought, I'd encourage you to remember that tall trees start as small seeds. Take an acorn for instance. An acorn can fit in the palm of your hand. But when planted in the right ground and nurtured properly, it will become an oak tree. Oak trees can grow forty-eight inches a year on average and can reach heights of eighty-two feet or more. Talk about a small beginning reaching great heights!

What if your marriage is in an acorn state? As you weigh your current predicament to the enormity of your relational potential, it may be discouraging. But every dream takes time, and it begins with being rooted in the right ground. Be faithful in leading your family God's way, and over time you'll grow strong, and leave a lasting legacy.

But you have to start somewhere, or change won't begin *anywhere*. Ask one another, what's our gifting? What are our unique abilities, perspectives, or services that we can offer the world? These questions must be answered in order to truly discover your dream.

I love this poem by Langston Hughes because it emphasizes the power of hopes and dreams:

> "Hold fast to dreams,
> For if dreams die
> Life is a broken-winged bird
> That cannot fly."

When we lose hope it's usually through a loss of vision. When we lack vision, we begin to experience a life without meaning. As Langston suggests, a bird is born to fly, but sadly it's stuck on the ground. When your dreams are delayed, your heart is unhealthy. Without a clear vision, you'll surely crash and burn. A lack of vision is like trying to drive your car with mud all over the windshield. You may be driving, but you're probably doing more damage than good. You're a danger to yourself and others because you can't see where you're going. Many people are like this in life, and that's why they're miserable. The day for driving with muddy windows is done! When you get a vision, a dream, a hope, you can see what's ahead and get to the destination.

Identifying Purpose Blockers

1. Recognize unhealthy family ties that keep you trapped.

Inherited family traits and traditions from our family can be positive, and in some ways, destructive. We are offspring from the roots of our family tree. There's no escaping the fact that people are the product of their environment. Just as we've received genetic similarities from family lines, we inherit behavioral tendencies as well. Some habits are positive, and others not so much. But we have to be careful of the mindset that accepts the norm because that's "just how we were raised." What if you were raised incorrectly? If you aren't careful, you'll settle for *what's always been* and miss the life *that could be.* Don't live at the level of your past limitations. Know this, what you tolerate as the way it is, will be, in one way or another, passed down from your generation to the next. Make a decision today to discover God's plan, so that you pass that down because His plan is what's best!

What's tricky about inherited beliefs is that they're hard to identify. We miss them because they're like contact lenses over our hearts. It's not a problem if the habit is healthy, but when it's not, we'll defend a culture that may be destructive. But this doesn't have to be the case in your home any longer. No matter what hardship you've experienced as a couple, you can be the generation that breaks the cycle and creates a new legacy. To plant healthy roots that produce fruit, you may have to pull up some unhealthy weeds.

To unearth the family ties that keep you trapped, start by processing the past biological influences. How has your marriage been shaped by the family systems you stem from? What are the positive memories of time spent with your family? Do you recall any painful moments while growing up that you've vowed never to allow to happen with your children? This may not be easy, but it needs to be done, so you can learn from the past and not repeat it in your future.

As you think back through these memories and experiences of life before marriage, are there any habits you formed? Were you a bright and talkative kid? Maybe something happened along the way, and you're not that way anymore. Or at least that's what you've grown to accept. Could it be that when you were excited and affectionate towards your family, they shut down your advances for affection? As a result, you've suppressed your true self. Your family lacks a level of expression and intimacy because the baggage from your old home moved into your new one.

Here's another example of how to discuss the good and the bad of the past as a couple. If you've realized that sexual dissatisfaction is increasing, what do you do? You need to process the past. Ask yourselves, was the use of pornography normalized in your family? Have you tried to introduce a desire into your bedroom inspired by porn? If so, you'll never be sexually satisfied while trying to emulate sex that was never designed for you. The best sex you'll ever have lies in your bed's safety. Your sexual identity should not be rooted in the corrupt ground of pornography. Neither should sex be displeasurable as a result of past sexual abuse. You may have been taken advantage of by a family member or assaulted and still desire to give yourself entirely to your spouse, but there's trauma that needs healing. Time won't heal these wounds. Neither will your silence.

If you've come from a family that was silent regarding sex talks, discussing any of this would be extremely uncomfortable. Growing up, just saying the word in our schools and home could get you into trouble. This culture of silence on the subject will keep you trapped in an unhealthy cycle. Since God created sex to be sacred and enjoyable, deal with anything that harms your intimacy. Creating a new culture in your home enables an open communication line where things can be dealt with as soon as possible. These conversations are possible with a couple that knows they're sexually pure in God's eyes. Despite the facts of previous harm caused by the misuse of sex, they are not what was done to them. They are not the sum of the mistakes they've made. They are God's children, chosen, forgiven, and free to forge a new sexual identity.

Don't wait to do something about dysfunctional cycles. Every year evaluate the soil around your roots to see if any weeds from the past spring up and choke the life out of your present. Set annual retreats (we'll discuss how to do this more in the next chapter) to process the past year. If you find any unhealthy habits that need to be trashed before heading into the future, how will you work together to get rid of them? Habits won't change themselves. You have to remove the old ways and replace them with new practices. What needs to change, and what's the plan to change them? Good question, but that question is not enough by itself. It all starts with answering the greater inquisition of your identity.

As a child, you may have accepted dysfunctional ways of thinking as you practiced what your family lived out as "normal behavior." From sitting in a room full of cigarette smoke to being around relatives addicted to drugs, or living with codependent parents, or seeing triggered angry outbursts. You may have lived with controlling parents, or quite possibly lived with no structure at all. This may be tough to do, but as you study generational cycles, you may realize that inadvertently, and unconsciously in some ways, you've perpetuated the past. What we're challenging you as a couple to fight for, is your right to determine what flows forward from now on, consciously.

We aren't suggesting a fishing expedition to blame your relatives for your pain. That will further reinforce and almost guarantee failure. We are saying to face the facts of your family. How did they become who they are? Could your family's path be more successful under different scenarios? If so, what healthy habits would have made the difference? It's literally like looking at a family tree. Only this time, it's as if you had the gift of seeing the spiritual genetics that contributed to this very season of your life. The decisions you make that shape your destiny are tied to the influence of your family.

2. Recognize your power to shape the future.

As we've discussed earlier in the book, you are a powerful couple, endowed with the precious gift of choice. Now more than ever, you should see why you must wield this power wisely. Our choices are connected to subconscious programming resulting in consequences that impact us further than what the moments of our decisions imply. Which is why this is so critical when in transition. *Transitions force decisions.* Since our choices stem from subconscious perceptions, we must carefully consider each one and see it as an extension of our identity. So, if you see yourselves as victorious, free people empowered by an All-mighty God, your life decisions flow from your Heavenly family. Imagine the choices you'll make for your future when deciding from this perspective. You're not weak victims of circumstance. You're influential, world-shaping individuals, choosing to leave a legacy of love in this world. One decision at a time is how you change your family line. Through combining your collective wisdom from the past, work together to build a loving, safe, prosperous, happy, and world-changing home.

It is true, you can't change the events of your family's past. But you can learn from them. To do this, you must be **aware** of them. After all, you can't fight an enemy you can't see. "Well, why don't we forget about the past and just start fresh." Running away may run you right into what you're fleeing. You've got to face the ugly facts, kill 'em with truth, and bury it in a deep grave far away from your new home. One of the greatest weapons given is the ability to choose healthy thoughts over another.

So how can you identify the real enemy? Spend some time reflecting and asking yourself these questions. Don't rush through them but allow yourself time to think, trace, and identify your roots. Look for problematic patterns. Are the same fault lines forming in your lives? Do the face morphs still trip you up? Are you clashing over the same money fights? Can't seem to find stability in your career? Does lust dominate your mind and cause your eyes to wander? Do you have the same disagreements on disciplining the kids? Are the same physical sicknesses resurfacing in your bodies? What mountain are you circling around as a couple every few years? What lessons have you learned, but can't seem to do any differently?

3. Pioneer your legacy.

You can be pioneers of new pathways if you pay attention to the patterns. Of course, solving puzzles gets easier when you have all of the pieces. To break free from being a prisoner of your past, you need a new definition of yourself. That definition comes from our Creator and flows through your family. When God speaks to your purpose, He simultaneously empowers you to perform it. If you're willing to agree with Him and accept His plan, He will establish His purpose through you. This happens as you take your will and surrender it to the power of His. If your life was a car, this is what it would look like: You, as the driver, releasing the wheel that directs the vehicle to the Lord's hands. More specifically, your *will* is the *wheel*, so hop out of the driver's seat altogether and let God direct your path. Lend Him your ears and submit your hands to Him. This is how you rise above the limitations of past hurts, habits, and hang-ups. Real change requires more than willpower. You ultimately need God's power. The awareness of His inheritance, traits, and culture that's readily available to all who will receive it.

In the last chapter, we covered surrender, and it's meaning. One of the reasons we find it harder to submit to one another is that we haven't fully surrendered our lives to God in certain areas. The truth about your husband will be discovered as you look into the face of your Heavenly Father. The reality that will give your wife happiness is found in the presence of His Spirit. Think of it this way, you received a physical nature from your earthly family: eye color, hair texture, and talents. But your personality, spirit, and character are inspired by the Heavenly One. The Bible says you're made in God's image. We are at our best then when we reflect Him to one another.

Hopefully, you can see why the fight for freedom isn't merely getting over the next hump. It's not just overcoming our various circumstances. This is about becoming a family that's rooted in the family tree of The Heavenly Father. Anything that pulls you away from that identity is the real enemy. You were born to produce love instead of fear, peace in place of anger. Joy, not depression. Prosperity over of poverty, patience rather than intolerance. If you want a home filled with these attributes, you must be connected to the True Vine. We're not talking about "*findin' religion.*" We're talking about developing a personal relationship with your loving Father who wants to live in you and flow out into your legacy. And in this family, there is a fullness of grace and truth. Here in this family, it's not about what you've done. It's about knowing who's you are. When you understand why God brought you and your spouse together, marriage gets better. With a target in sight, you're propelled by purpose, collectively moving in the same direction as one plate without fault lines. When you build on the foundation of your Heavenly Father, lasting change begins to take place.

Yes, you may have come from a home where angry outbursts were a way of life. Maybe that's the best that they could do with what they knew. But in your marriage, God is at the center. He's not angry with you, and He sets the example of your attitude with one another. If your spouse is not doing what you want or hearing what you're saying, God's long-suffering character rules in your heart. As a result, you know that patience is the pathway. As you feel frustration rising within, you call a time out, take a walk away from the talk, and calmly return thirty minutes later. Having prayed to your Father during your stroll around the block, He gently speaks to you. In doing so, you're reminded that you're not alone. Simultaneously as He speaks, you're empowered by your source, and so you return with a renewed mind. You don't have to control the situation because you're in conversation with the One who does. With authority, you calmly resist the urge to yell. Realizing it yields results contrary to your new identity—a peacemaker, like the Prince of Peace. There, right there at that moment, you are walking in true freedom.

You might have been raised in a home where kind words weren't spoken. Maybe your family never really expressed through words their love and affirmation to one another. As a result, your heart is hardened to saying, "I love you." You may say, "Why do I have to say it when I can just show it?" To that, I say, why not communicate your love through both words and actions? Your children need to hear your verbal affirmation. The words you speak give the family life. In this place of freedom, you communicate acceptance, appreciation, and affection through what you do and the words you say. Where you've come from may have shaped you to think that words are mushy, unnecessary, or they should just "know." But what did your Heavenly Father do over His son Jesus? Before Jesus ever accomplished any ministry work, He was affirmed through words from His Heavenly Daddy. And in Matthew 3:17, a voice from heaven said, *"This is my dearly loved Son, who brings me great joy."*

Jesus conducted His activity from the root of an affirmed identity. No wonder Jesus gave Himself to redeem His family. He knew intimately the example of love conveyed through His Father. This is why a new culture is essential to forge a new and life-giving legacy. In clinging to the ways of old, you participate in a plan that's less than God's best, and you'll perpetuate hardened hearts instead of loving-kindness. Let this transition you're in expose some areas that need internal growth. Instead of asking God, "Why did this happen?" allow the transition to teach you about yourself as it reveals triggers that keep setting your relationship backward.

Have you normalized negative habits? Many couples want better lives, but they continue to accept mediocrity as a perpetual mindset. Some settle for an average marriage—complying with cycles that keep us chained—but your marriage can change from a mess to a masterpiece, from average to excellent. Excellence means doing the best you can with the best that you have. Since God is magnificent, and you have access to Him, your home should shine brightly with excellence.

4. Maximize the power of prayer.

In the Reed home, we can directly link specific prayer requests for our greatest desires to supernatural fulfillment. Throughout our twenty-four-year history, God has never failed to show Himself strong in our moments of weakness. Prayer not only changes things, but it changes *us*. It's amazing how many couples have witnessed the miraculous as a result of a faith-filled request, but still find it challenging to grab hands with their closest friend—their spouse—to speak with our Heavenly Father. Whether it's out of pride, embarrassment, or in some cases, laziness, couples don't pray out loud, nor often enough. How often is often enough? The answer is, as much as you desire to be close to God and each other.

A lack of prayer leads to stunted potential. If you want to grow beyond temporal change, prayer is essential. I'm not talking about fancy words or long religious sound bites. I'm talking about transparency in His presence. Praying until you're awakened to an awareness of His closeness—until you know He's with you in the room. His presence makes all the difference. I don't know where you are in your walk with God. I know that a consistent prayer life draws you closer to the Father, which translates to a healthier version of self. If you've fallen away from intimate chats with God, begin again today. In fact, you can start right now. He's waiting. I believe He's been expecting you with loving arms that are ready to embrace you. He's not looking for perfectly written prayers. He simply longs for honest talks from surrendered hearts.

When you acknowledge His presence, He empowers your performance. Just knowing that you're secure in The Savior heals you on so many levels. Time with God refuels your joy, peace, and love. He sufficiently satisfies our souls. Afterward, we're not desperate for our spouses to fill the voids within us that only **God** can fill. That's a huge weight lifted off of their shoulders. When they don't have to "make you happy" because you're already content in Christ, it eliminates pressure.

On another level, when you come out of prayer, you don't forget that God is still there. You don't forget that you're responsible to God for how you honor your spouse. I mean, would you disrespect your spouse if Jesus was sitting next to you on a couch? Even if you would be so bold to do so, would you not apologize after coming to your senses? After all, you stand in the presence of the One who paid the penalty for your sin. Who are you then to throw stones at another when God has none left to chunk at you?

Wouldn't you extend grace to your precious spouse while beholding the face of The Father? Oswald Chambers wrote that "Prayer is the exercise of drawing on the grace of God." Every marriage could use an abundance of grace. Too many marriages fall apart because they lack the glue that holds them together. It's you two plus God at the center. God brought the woman out of the man; He then stood in the middle and gave the miracle of marriage. Without Him in the center, guiding our thoughts and flowing through our actions, we lack the power to produce a healthy home.

When you realize He is always with you, you can then lean on Him to guide you through any transition your marriage may face. Let your heart rest in the consistency of our Heavenly Father. Let His love and faithfulness be the pillow your heart can rest on. Be still and allow Him to share with you the truth of who you are and why you're together.

Set a time and a place to tune in to God's voice. If you're wondering what His leading sounds like, well He sounds like love, kindness, gentleness, patience, and self-control. In Galatians 5:22-23, Paul describes the attributes and personality of God and The Holy Spirit:

But what happens when we live God's way? He brings gifts into our lives, much the same way that fruit appears in an orchard— things like affection for others, exuberance about life, serenity. We develop a willingness to stick with things, a sense of compassion in the heart, and a conviction that a basic holiness permeates things and people. We find ourselves involved in loyal commitments, not needing to force our way in life, able to marshal and direct our energies wisely. Legalism is helpless in bringing this about; it only gets in the way. Among those who belong to Christ, everything connected with getting our own way and mindlessly responding to what everyone else calls necessities is killed off for good—crucified (MSG).

His thoughts become the governing voice that guides your life. He'll never lead you towards thoughts that are contrary to His character. But the above verses are a picture of the influence of His personality at work within our own. Imagine that passage was a description of God's Kingdom flowing through you to your family. As you pray—His Kingdom come and will be done—follow His lead, and you'll experience a win. These are small victories, as a result of conscious choices and moments of surrender, reshape your trajectory. They slowly but surely break painful and unhealthy cycles. It will all be worth it when your children see patience displayed while you're dealing with them. They will learn as you model self-control in stressful moments. As they watch intense moments bring you together instead of tearing you apart, they see teamwork over selfishness. They simultaneously learn a way of creating a better world.

In the next chapter, we'll share practical tips that show you how to keep your eyes on the big picture and build a family legacy when the world seems to be falling apart.

CHAPTER TAKEAWAYS:

1. Name a few purpose blockers you identified with as you were reading this chapter.

2. Have you maximized the power of prayer in your marriage? Have you prayed with one another or prayed over your marriage purpose?

3. If not, will you make a decision to do so together?

NEW EXPECTATIONS FOR FUTURE PLACES

9

The Big Picture

"Legacy is not leaving something for people.
It's leaving something in people."

—PETER STROPLE

CREATING A GENERATIONAL LEGACY TAKES GRIT. IT REQUIRES A determined husband and wife to hammer into society a culture of good success. It requires a couple so focused on future generations that they are unshaken by temporary circumstances. When they face problems, they don't put their legacy on pause. They keep their eyes on the big picture. In doing so, they create generational wealth so transcendent that their children's children will build on their foundation. All because they endure the pain of tough transitions by keeping their eyes on a bigger vision and legacy. Just as businessman Gary Vaynerchuk said, "Please think about your legacy because you are writing it every day."

Every day that you are breathing is a gift. Time is the most precious commodity that you have. Due to the fact that once it's gone, you can't recover it. You can earn more money, purchase another house, and get new clothes, but once the time is gone, there is no going back. Your children will only be toddlers and teenagers for so long. You have to live in such a way that you steward well the true wealth—your family. Your twenties will soon be your sixties. When you look back over the decades, what will you have done with the days gone by?

Live in such a way that says, "I must make each day count!" Keeping the big picture in mind means you dream a destiny so big that it outlives you. This dream should inspire you to accomplish more than your ancestors. You are adding to, and simultaneously changing your entire family line. If your marriage is a tree, you want the roots to run deep so that future generations rise and produce Kingdom fruit. Your marriage becomes a conduit for Kingdom blessing. What does that destiny look like for you? You've got to dream it and write the vision down on paper!

For our home, we turned to The Bible and discovered a passage of scripture that embodied the legacy that we'd like to leave. We call it The Family Legacy Statement, and it's our vision. The big picture that we're working hard to create. Oh, and by the way, if you like it, you can use it too. I don't think God minds if we share it. Psalm 112:

Praise the Lord! How joyful are those who fear the LORD and delight in obeying his commands. Their children will be successful everywhere; an entire generation of godly people will be blessed. They themselves will be wealthy, and their good deeds will last forever. Light shines in the darkness for the godly. They are generous, compassionate, and righteous. Good comes to those who lend money generously and conduct their business fairly. Such people will not be overcome by evil. Those who are righteous will be long remembered. They do not fear bad news; they confidently trust the Lord to care for them. They are confident and fearless and can face their foes triumphantly. They share freely and give generously to those in need. Their good deeds will be remembered forever. They will have influence and honor. The wicked will see this and be infuriated. They will grind their teeth in anger; they will slink away, their hopes thwarted.

Man, that's good stuff! After swapping out "those, they, their, and such people" for our names, this passage got personal. It's the perfect description of not only what we'd love to see as a result of our marriage, but also what we'd be proud to witness in our future generations. What would you like to see as a result of your union? Dream it and write it down. A written vision resets your sights to what's most important. It reminds you why you're willing to stay in the fight for your family when things aren't going so well.

If you could take the Reed's heart and put it under a microscope, this is at the center of our desires for you too. That the goodness of God overtakes you regardless of the season your family finds itself within. That even in the worst of transitions, His Kingdom would flow in you and through you to transform darkness to light. That your home reflects the beauty of Heaven in a sometimes-ugly world, and your marriage stands as a testament of unconditional love. That is our hope and prayer for you all. This will take work to accomplish, but if you're both willing to put in the effort, it's well worth it. If you want to achieve your big picture, here are a few areas of priority to help you frame the home you desire.

Focus on Your Own Home

Comparison is a home-wrecker. Wishing your spouse was like someone else kills your contentment. They've been created in the image of God, and that should be admirable enough. Find the gold in your own home because what you're chasing somewhere else may turn out to be fool's gold. Sure, the grass may look greener in everyone else's marriage, but you don't know what manure it took to get them there. It's great that your parents have a fantastic friendship. It's terrific that you're connected to a couple at church you admire or a mentor you aspire to emulate. So long as you remember, you're not them. You can only walk the path of God's plan for *you*. And honestly, that's what makes your journey special. You can leave your unique fingerprint in this world. Don't waste your days envying a cheap imitation of something that may not even be authentic. On the outside, they may look the part, but you don't know what's truly in their hearts. If you focus on your own home, it takes less energy to be authentic to embrace the reality of who you are as a couple.

Release the need to have the so-called "perfect marriage." Perfection is a mirage that'll leave you thirsty. Meanwhile, in reality, you're surrounded by an ocean titled "just right" for each other. Contentment will kill comparison, and peace lies on the other side of a grateful heart. Learning to appreciate your family as they are not as you wish them to be is the key. Take a moment to thank God for them during your prayer time. Expressing daily admiration softens your heart and shifts your perspective. When you have people to be grateful for, you'll discover you have something to be thankful for. Within this space of contentment, it's easier to cast every fault, flaw, and frailty of your imperfect family into the hands of a perfect God. Trust Him to handle the healing of your home.

Find Your Grit

Tough times aren't hard to find, but tough people are. Couples with grit face all manner of adversity, and yet, they remain unshaken in their convictions. They find a way to persevere, push through, and make progress through difficult transitions. Instead of being broken by shifts, they eventually break through to new levels. That is what we need in America and all around the world—amid pandemics, political unrest, economic uncertainty, and only God knows what else—couples who remain undeterred. We need couples that are pressing forward passionately towards their destination. Adapting as needed to create traditions that outlast their transitions. Those who'll face head-on whatever the world throws at them and won't quit because they know they're too important to fail, and because they know there's only a short amount of time to leave a great legacy in this world, they don't waste the present wandering around the same mountains of broken dreams and dysfunctional behavior.

How do you find your grit? **Remember. Your. Why**. At one point, I, Sean, was about sixty pounds overweight. When I began my weight loss journey, I had a motivational statement that I kept in front of me. I answered the question, "Why can't you stay the way that you are?" It changed my life! My answer was written on an old picture of my body at its healthiest. The answers flowed without hesitation. I can't stay in this unhealthy cycle because I want to run with my grandkids someday; I don't like getting winded while going up a flight of stairs; The pain in my knees and back will be alleviated if I lose weight; My body is God's temple, and I should invest in it. These answers outweighed the work that I'd have to put in. I put together a plan, and every day I'd grind forward until I made it through my weight transformation. Clearly define your own personal why. When you're fully convinced that you belong in the relationship and that your life is jam-packed with meaning, it strengthens your will to move forward. Where can you write it down and keep it where you can see it? When life gets hard, and the transitions suck, take ten minutes to cry and complain. Then pull yourself together, and wipe the tears from your eyes. Cast your cares to God, course correct as needed, and keep going. Find your grit, and keep grinding forward.

You may be thinking, *Well, you guys don't understand how bad things are for us right now*. Trust us, we get it. It's hard to make lemonade in life when all you see are sour lemons and no apparent sweetness. It's downright deflating. If you're at a point where you don't feel motivated, you've got to keep it moving. One thing's for certain, you'll never gain traction where there's no action. Find the place where your passions and purpose collide and engage in activities that jumpstart motivation.

Think of your marriage as a marathon rather than a sprint. If you've ever run long-distance, you know one thing's for certain, you've got to commit. Twenty-six point two miles or about fifty thousand steps only happen when you put one foot in front of the other. Ultimately, it takes a deep determination to control one's mind and body through to the finish line. Many people, however, sign up for races and never show up. On their record, it gets stamped "did not finish." If you're intent on finishing your course and finishing strong, then work yourself into motivation. Don't wait on a feeling, your spouse, or circumstances to improve. Now that you're rooted in purpose and aware of your life's meaningfulness, start placing one foot in front of the other toward your why.

Plan an Annual Vision Retreat

Retreat to a mountain you've never seen. Or a Motel 6 up the road if that's what is available in the budget. Just get away to a place where you can dream together. Here is a moment to get in sync. We highly encourage you to check out this subscription service by XO Marriage: now.xomarriage.com/vision-retreat-journey to help you on your retreat. To hone in on future goals, aspirations, wants, and needs, we like to plan ours towards the end of the year. It gives time to share our thoughts about what worked over the last year and what went so terribly wrong that it shouldn't happen again. We share the vision. Typically, we look beyond the next year, venturing out as far as the next five years.

This is a time to leave the kids behind. Find someone who'll ease your mind about their safety and well-being. They'll survive for a few days. Leave work at the office. Make this a special moment to process the past and plan the future. Design the big picture. Since we've committed to making time for annual vision retreats, we've noticed we've exceeded our goals, and we've grown closer through the years.

Before leaving for our retreat, we take two copies of questions for us to answer separately. After we'd spent time in prayer and reflection, we come together to see if we were on the same page. If we're not, we talk it out until we agree on which course to take. We ask questions like: What's God saying for our financial future? How should we pray for our children specifically? Where would we like to travel as a family over the next three to five years? How much should we give this year above our tithe as an offering? Is there a mistake that we made this last year, and what did we learn from it?

Sean and I do this every year and have been doing this for the past ten years. I can honestly say that it was one of the game-changers in our marriage. Due to our children's school schedules, we were only able to slip away for a couple of days. In hindsight, I honestly feel those are the best times. Relaxing in a quiet hotel restaurant completely relaxed, we'd casually chat. Taking in the drama of the hotel decor, we get inspired and commence to dreaming again. Enjoying one another's presence as we soak in the unfamiliar sights of downtown streets in a city we've never seen. And of course, having lots of sex. It gives us an opportunity to reprioritize plans that may have been pushed aside and bring them back to life.

After coming into agreement on what we believe God has spoken and what we've expressed from our hearts' desires, we combine those answers to one sheet. That becomes our vision for the next year. From here, we formalize actionable goals with timelines for execution. After all, dreams are just wishful thinking without a deadline and actionable items to accomplish them. Let's say you both agree that it's time for a family vacation. That's great, now what? Is the purpose for recuperation, leisure times, or fun? Where are you headed to, and what's the exact date of departure? How much of the monthly budget can we invest? Can you put together an itinerary of the activities and tours you'll take once you arrive at your destination? Vision becomes a reality when your goals get to work.

Say you both sense a need for quality time as a family. Excellent! What would it take for this year to be different than the last one? Write down what quality time means practically. If you see that as game nights, get everyone involved, ask them what their favorite games are, and set a scheduled day with rotating games. Maybe intimate discussions fit your definition. Try finding the right questions to generate stimulating conversations. Once a week, carve out time to get creative ideas that foster community, but I cannot emphasize enough the need to schedule quality time with the *entire* family. A family schedule that syncs all activities from each family member may give an overview that helps you figure out the best time. The point here is that your yearly goals break down into monthly agendas that must be converted to daily deposits towards your dream. You can either *wish* for a better marriage and family or *work* towards building one!

Plan the Budget Together

Money fights in marriage are major. It's challenging enough to handle finances by yourself, let alone with another person whose tendencies, opinions, and habits differ from your own. Add to that a crisis of sickness, job layoffs, or new braces for the kiddos, and it's all the more stressful. To alleviate, at the very least, rising tension between each other, transparency is vital. Communication and equal participation in financial planning are essential. There are many resources out there like Financial Peace University and Crown Financial that offer courses on managing money as a team. Our two cents on the matter is this: the big picture requires some green paper. And if you don't agree on the direction of your dollars, a division is sure to follow. Setting a monthly meeting where you both show up, share your thoughts, and see the numbers is a must. We encourage you to agree on a date to meet together. You'll never accomplish the big picture if you push away your partner. They need you to commit, to be present, and to participate willingly. Don't let one person carry the load of creating the budget without your input. Share your thoughts because you need to buy into the plan. It doesn't help in the long run if they've crunched the numbers, and you crush it by doing your own thing with your debit card. When you meet up once a month and see what's happening, you can quickly make adjustments to avoid falling into destructive habits that hinder your prosperity.

In our partnership, I, Lanette, enjoy crunching numbers. I consider myself everyone's assistant in the home. Making it my business to know all the details of who needs to do what by when. I break out my spreadsheets with dogged determination to balance the budget, and then I present the numbers to Sean as his strength is to sniff out things I may have missed. Realizing I'm not perfect, I'm open to receiving his insight. Initially, I was a reluctant receiver of hearing and receiving his input. It took time to develop a sense of trust and find security in what he had to say. The financial mistakes we encountered in the past left bruises. I figured if I could control the money, then I could secure our financial situation, but unity in marriage doesn't work like that. With transparency and healing, we began the process of overcoming those bruises.

Financial stress has been linked to health problems, reduced overall productivity, and it strains the relationship. Many Americans don't live on a budget, and for those that do, they find it challenging to stick with the numbers they've created. You, my friend, have a built-in accountability partner. This scheduled meeting can become a time of motivation or revelation. Motivation because you're actually winning as you're working towards your big picture. Revelation in that you may need to make severe changes because you're not gaining any traction toward the vision—but that's a good thing. People spend years of their lives doing the same things and getting the same results. But this won't be the case for you. Why? Because you'll catch it while you're seeing the numbers, sharing your thoughts in the meeting you showed up for.

Plan a Weekly Tune-up

As you're multitasking the many day-to-day challenges of life, make time to meet with your spouse about essential matters. Take about forty-five minutes for uninterrupted, kid, and smart device-free, off time. Find a comfortable, quiet place to tune-up your teamwork. Depending on your schedule, the day and time may need to adjust accordingly. But at the very least, once per week. "Why should we meet every week?" For starters, it enables you to:

1. Prevent small match fires from evolving into huge flames that potentially burn the house down in the future. You nip the conflict in the bud before it becomes a crisis.
2. Release potential resentment. Instead of living with pent-up aggression stemming from misunderstandings, you make efforts to resolve issues.
3. Have peace of mind over time because closure comes more consistently.

As discussed earlier in this book, you may want to jot down your thoughts regarding the one issue you'd like to focus on at a time. In preparation for the meeting, write out something you appreciate about your spouse. This way, when you kick off the session, you're not popping off insults. Remember, genuine praise paves the way for an open discussion of a problem. It's important to note that this meeting doesn't have to be stressful. You're not confronting an enemy, even if you are discussing problematic behavior. Talking about a problem isn't disrespecting a person.

Speak to them with humility and love. They are still your friend and lover, so your tone throughout the meeting should reflect this. Don't see it as a daunting task that you *have* to do. Know that it's an opportunity for increased unity that you *get* to do. It's making you better, so to the best of your ability, try and keep the atmosphere as positive as possible.

This tune-up prevents engine failure in the future. Since healthy things eliminate waste, these meetings serve to celebrate the good and eliminate internal congestion. When people hold things in, it eats away at them. Sometimes they hold things in for years that could be handled in minutes. If they have pit stops where they pull over on the track, they could quickly recover and get back out on the road. Instead, they eventually explode or implode due to unmet expectations.

You can also use this time to touch base on any unmet needs. Do you need to tweak the chores around the house? Speak up if you need more support with one of your children's behavioral issues? Should you schedule a time for sex because well... it's been a while? Are you feeling ignored? If so, how can they practically recognize you in a meaningful way?

As you connect more regularly, the meetings typically run smoother and move a little faster. The more you mature, you take things less personal as well. Your marriage becomes a well-oiled machine that's successfully navigating the transitions of life.

Plan Weekly Date-Time

I'm sure you've heard by now that couples need a date night. If you didn't know, now you do. But what if you don't have a *night* for a date? Conflicting work schedules, finding childcare workers, and fatigue create real challenges. One spouse may be a homebody while the other needs a night on the town. Meet these challenges head-on! Put your brilliant minds together to carve out a time that works well for you. If a weekly breakfast is all you can commit to, then find ways to make it unique. Realize also that some people aren't the most spontaneous. Others don't specialize in event planning, so if your longing for them to flex a muscle they're weak in, you'll be disappointed. What we suggest is that you generate a list of date-time ideas to choose from. Search for events happening in your town, and list them by date and time. Send the list over to your significant other and let them pick what works for them. Your date-time may even be a walk in the park together. Sitting on the beach or...well, I think you get the point.

Whatever you choose to do, make sure to actually do it. It's all about prioritizing your friendship and keeping the flame of romance lit. Getting to know them on a deeper level and reminding yourself that they're not old news. There's still more to explore in their hearts if you have the time to look. Here's an important tip: as you get all sexy for your mate, prepare for your date. Get a few questions that will stimulate conversation. We're not saying that everything has to be all structured. Hey, if you're good with a free-flowing night on the town, that's great. But if you struggle to find the words to say, it may be because you've lost the right questions to ask. When this happens, the time you spend together may only serve as a reminder of how far you've grown apart. With a little preparation to generate stimulating conversation, you may find your way back to one another. Time away from the kids and work allows your mind to get away from the drama long enough to remember why you fell in love with them in the first place.

Plan for Romance

In 2009, a survey was conducted on the importance of romance in a relationship. Some forty-two percent of respondents stated that romance was essential to them in a relationship because they could not feel love without it. Nineteen percent say that it's important at the beginning of the relationship in order to establish it. Ten percent say it's only useful for getting what you want from the other person and five percent say it's not important. [9]

Where do you land in that survey? Maybe you find yourself in the forty-two percent of folks who think that it's essential to feeling love. To you, romance instigates a connection that communicates relational worth and value. Without it, the relationship lacks a key factor to keep the flame of love burning brightly. From your perspective, romance is a test of commitment and priority. Until you speak through this language, you're really not saying you care at all. Sure, your mouth may occasionally say that you love them, but your unromantic habits tell a different tale.

Perhaps you stumbled into the nineteen percent that believe romance is a temporary phase. It got the ball rolling and now it's game on. Marriage is business as usual. Puppy love had its place, but let's get real, we don't live in a fairytale. You should know by now that I love you, and we can live without all of the stereotypical antiquated ideas of childish gestures. Sadly, some believe that romance is merely a tool for flattery designed to appease your spouse by checking boxes of couple's compliance on a special holiday. To others, it's a quid-pro-quo, cleverly wielded in exchange for sex. This disparity in seeing the value of romance within relationships has us persuaded that we must dive deeper to unearth the truth of its necessity.

We've developed our own definition of romance. *It's the attitude of love expressed in words and actions.* Attitudes are the way we've settled into thinking or feeling about a person, but our moods are the result of our perspective of life in general. Some spouses wake

---

9. AARP Knowledge Management, G. Oscar Anderson, "Love, Actually: A National Survey of Adults 18+ on Love, Relationships, and Romance." (AARP, November 1, 2009), https://www.aarp.org/relationships/love-sex/info-11-2009/love_09.html.

up on the wrong side of the bed every day. Like grown-up versions of Pigpen from Charlie Brown. A cloud of dusty drama surrounds them, and it's often difficult to contain their negativity on the inside. When someone is in a bad mood, you can see and sense it in their body language. And out of the mood of their heart, their mouth will soon speak. Conversely, positive emotions about a person emerge from beneath the surface and are expressed through healthy touch, compliments, sexual intimacy, and thoughtfulness.

How do you generally feel about your spouse? Your words and actions will more than likely follow your attitude towards them. If you think highly of them, the chances are you will be more willing to share romance. Sure, there are many outside influences, and in the case of this book, transitions that may affect your overall frequency of expressing love, like chronic health problems. Still, the person whose attitude is in favor of their spouse and the marriage is one of positivity, and that gives hope to romantic possibilities.

If your attitude is rooted in unresolved hurt, bitterness, or anger, what are the chances that you'll express exactly what's in your heart? I'd say pretty low. When a person believes a spouse to be the cause of their unhappiness, they draw back from the source of pain. This would be unromantic, cold-natured, isolated, and emotionally disconnected. If there's a lack of healthy touch, intimate conversation, or romantic expressions, attitudes definitely need to be adjusted. That relationship must find its way to demonstrable love. And this, my friends, is an investment of time, money, and energy. The effort you put into romance is to show them you care about them in the ways they have shared makes them happy.

Sometimes, there are also attitudes of genuine love for the spouse that are not expressed, simply because it's not the style of one person in the relationship. The entire culture of romantic gestures may seem mushy, unnecessary, or like a waste of money. The hindrance here is one person's preference or both spouses, in some cases, avoid a certain level of vulnerability. In a sense, they simply refuse to participate. I've seen so many great marriages go down unnecessarily because of an unwillingness to supply what the other person was desperately in need of. A great marriage gets suffocated by a lack of intimacy when romance is the very oxygen that would've given it life.

Romance selflessly expresses care for your spouse in ways they interpret as prioritized care on a daily basis. Now, given our definition of romance, and hopefully, a newfound perspective, let me ask you a question, are you a romantic person? The answer should be yes! Say it with me, my non-mushy friends, *I will selflessly express care towards my spouse in the ways they consider loving.*

Maybe before this moment, you viewed romance as a holiday card or box of candy given on a special occasion. But if you're the type who sees cards as a waste of paper, that flowers belong in the ground where they grow and are also allergic to candy, it simply doesn't mesh. But from our definition, you can see that it's so much more than clichéd gifts. It's there in the gentle foot massage offered after a hard day's work. Displayed through attentive ears readily listening to stimulating conversation. For every marriage, it can and should be exchanged because you love them.

Love is an action word that calls us to serve others in ways we'd like to be treated. It's doing what's right to those who may not offer you the same courtesy. It gives an abundance of grace for flawed people because relationship precedes behavior. Love is the bedrock from which all romantic deeds flow. It's a powerful force that's able to comfort your spouse when they're hurting and esteem them to greatness.

It starts with the gratitude in your heart and flows into their prescribed desire for physical connection. One of the foremost expressions of love is your words. Let's say you had a recorder in your pocket throughout this last day, week, or month. Would your spouse say that your words have been romantic? When time with you is less than kind because well, you aren't being kind, flowers don't really mean much. Sex may be a struggle, and to some, unenjoyable when there's no joy in just being around you.

What people really need before great gift ideas is someone who's been *for* them on a daily basis. Someone who acknowledges their efforts to look nice through a compliment. Or if you'll pause while you're at work to send a simple text message like, "Just thinking about when we first met, and I'm still in love with you." Gestures that solidify your spouse's priority in your life. Assuring them, they have a warm heart looking out for them in a very cold world. It's not unusual to hear people spread negativity and dish out overly critical speeches; it seems to flow out effortlessly. Whereas saying something nice, especially about their spouse in trying times, is seemingly hard for people to do.

See romance is like hydration to a marathon runner along their difficult journey. There are some dehydrated couples in desperate need of refreshing. Make an effort to say what they need to hear and allow your actions to express what's truly in your heart towards your spouse. Leave no doubt in the mind of your spouse about how much they mean to you.

Plan Memorable Vacations

Once you say, "I do," it can seem like life takes off. Managing money, raising children, busy schedules, and all of your responsibilities attach strings to each spouse. As the demands increase, these strings tend to pull us apart. So, making time to detach yourself from the drama helps you re-establish a sense of closeness.

Even if you're not interested in traveling the world, we'd like to challenge you to step out of your comfort zone and try it. There's something special about being on an adventure with your family. Whether it's a road trip to a nearby city or flying to a destination around the world, it strengthens your family bond. I can't fully explain it, but I know this to be true. Every time our family travels together, we create memories. To this day, we bring up hilarious stories that we reminisce on from a decade ago. It instantly creates new laughter from old times. Times we would never have if we didn't make time, set aside resources, and create memorable moments.

In our family of five, we rarely agree on where we'd like to eat, which city we'd visit, or even the activities we do upon arrival. It's a tough task to get everyone excited about a trip. Especially since they're all adults now with fully formed opinions and packed agendas, it's still worth working through egos and personality clashes. Prioritizing quality time communicates value. We are pausing the drama to preserve the dream. To refresh relationships, bonds, and explore the world is so worth it.

A few tips on taking trips with your family:

1. Share trip details as soon as possible. The sooner you can share information with the entire family, the better.
2. When feasible, allow everyone to contribute ideas and share feedback on what to do when you get there. If you have children, use vacations as teachable moments. There's so much they can learn if you're not too hands-on.
3. Give them a little freedom in choosing what to pack. Have them check-in for a flight, use a map to navigate new cities, and pay the bill at restaurants themselves. It's a great way for them to mature and learn responsibility through real-world experiences.
4. Try not to over-plan the trip. Leave room for relaxation and reflection. An overpacked schedule may leave you and the entire family exhausted.
5. If you're on a tight budget, you can still take exceptional trips. Find coupons, discounts, and take advantage of sales. Remember, there are no victims allowed.

When we were struggling financially, we said things like, "We can't afford to go on vacation," or we'd say, "We don't have the time to go on a trip." What we know now is that we can't live without them. That if we set our minds to it and a little bit of money, we can make it happen. One of our family trips when we lived in Fort Worth, Texas, was a two-day staycation in Dallas. It's literally 30 minutes away. It didn't cost us much in gas, and we found a hotel. We created a schedule of visiting as many free museums as possible—tried food from places that served family-style with coupons that knocked down the price. We had a great time. At one point, we pulled out an old-fashioned map and had our kids navigate downtown Dallas's streets. They'd never really seen one let alone used a physical map. It was hilarious, and we'll always remember our staycation. Don't let money be the reason you fail to create memorable trips as a family. Get off the couch and get creative. Go out and see the world with the people who matter most in your life.

There's a word that was used throughout this chapter that's extremely important: **Create**. We're highlighting create because it's really up to you to customize the tools of this chapter. Together as a team, you make the big picture happen. It will work if *you* work it. Don't passively allow your dreams to waste away. It's great to pray and believe God's will over your family, but until you live out the priorities of your prayers, it won't happen. John Maxwell, one of our favorite authors, wrote a small book that really changed our lives titled, *Make Today Count*. In the book, he says, "Neglect enough todays, and you'll experience the "someday" you've wanted to avoid." Don't be the family that procrastinates on your purpose. Make a proactive choice to take the initiative towards your dreams today.

CHAPTER TAKEAWAYS

1. How can you show romance to your spouse today?

2. Out of the suggestions listed, what two things can you begin to make plans for?

3. What ways can you remind yourself to show love and romance to your spouse?

10

Leadership in Relationships

*"We don't want to settle for a good marriage, we
want to do what it takes to have a great marriage."*

—PASTOR AARON KENNEDY

HEY GUYS, IT'S SEAN HERE. A THOUGHT CAME TO MIND WHILE
completing this book. And it was this: Every husband and wife,
by default, is a leader. They are called to chart the course of the
unknown as a unified team. I'm a die-hard fan of Clifton Strengths
Assessments. One of my top five strengths is "Learner". Suffice it to
say, I've read a lot of books, especially resources regarding leadership.
In all my years of study, I haven't come across many that delve into
this idea of *leadership in relationships*.

With so many lessons on the subject, I initially hesitated to
include my two cents on the matter, but I couldn't shake it. I find it
amazing that people may be exceptional managers in the workplace.
And as contract talks stall, they somehow creatively figure out how
to close the deal. Should the equipment malfunction, their ingenuity
kicks into high gear and manage to create a workaround to proceed

forward. But when they get home, that very same solution-oriented, team-playing person takes a backseat to conflict. Maybe it's a matter of fatigue, or it could be that on some level, they're allowing discouragement to direct the intensity of their leadership.

Here's the thing, you are responsible for the stewardship of your relationship. Marriage doesn't achieve greatness on autopilot. You have to collectively map out plans that pave the way to a great life. In other words, things won't get better if you don't. Growth doesn't just magically transpire; it is acquired. Leadership is like a muscle that needs a healthy diet and exercise to build it up and maintain the best shape possible. Some couples haven't been to the gym of leadership development in a while.

What's stunting the growth of initiative may be the feeding of a victim's mentality. Feeling sorry for yourself or the unfavorable circumstances of your family changes nothing for the better. You are in charge and have been granted authority to take action.

Mature, high-caliber leaders take control of unfortunate events, whereas victims blame everyone else for their pain. Not realizing that as they walk with this helpless mentality, little by little, it's diminishing their strength. The more they look into the mirror, frustration with stagnation fosters a culture of dissatisfaction. Oftentimes, fumes of anger surge beneath the surface and eventually manifest once again with finger-pointing for their personal problems. "It's my wife's fault we lost our home. She wasn't even trying to help pay the bills." "My husband's always blowing up over little things, and it makes me so mad that it provokes me!" And the merry go round continues on and on. How will change ever come if no one takes control?

All people, on some level, have bouts with blame. It's part of our fallen nature. We see failed attempts at life or behaviors we disapprove and call out their character, without taking in the full context of the circumstances surrounding what we saw. In marriage, this is tough because you're constantly reading into the things your spouse tends to do. What I suggest when the blame-game comes-a-knocking at your door is to own your personal response and responsibility. Take ownership of any role you may have played in creating the challenging circumstance at hand. Even if they don't admit to their contribution, refuse to add another log to the fire. Why? Because you're a healthy, high caliber leader on the way to a great destination. You don't have time to play the blame-game. It's like little kids going back and forth on the playground: "I know you are, but what am I?" It stops today. What I am is responsible for are my own actions—willing to own my part and willing to go so far as to help them accomplish theirs. Mature couples face their problems, knowing they have the power to choose a pathway forward. Accepting the charge to make the necessary choices required to prosper. It's easy to point the finger at someone else and say, "This is all your fault." It takes courage to walk in accountability. Because you'll have to admit when you were wrong without following that up with how your spouse was as well. Are you ready to let go of your ego? If so, then you're ready to grow.

Helen Keller said, "Self-pity is our worst enemy and if we yield to it, we can never do anything good in the world." When Keller was born, she could see and hear but lost both abilities when she was eighteen months old due to a high fever from an unknown illness. She became blind and deaf. Very few people believed that a person in her condition would achieve anything significant in life. Yet, Helen proved that the deaf and blind could learn, graduate from college, write books, and change the world.

She was the most unlikely of heroes, and given her beginning, many wouldn't call her great. Her family could've given up on her. She could've fallen prey to self-pity and excuses. She could've complained about being dealt an unfair hand in life. If anyone could say that they didn't have a great beginning, it was Helen. But this woman grew to be respected and admired by presidents— actually meeting every president from Grover Cleveland to John

Kennedy—actors, and the blind and deaf people of the world. She traveled across the country making speeches and creating organizations for the blind. She won an Oscar and was awarded the Congressional Medal of Honor.

As in the life of Helen Keller, we'll all face opposition. We'll have hurdles to overcome in order to leave a great legacy. Our circumstances are all different. In Helen's case, it was an extreme disability, but she overcame with the help of great teachers and leaders. What's your excuse, reason, or justification as to why your marriage hasn't achieved greatness? Write out that excuse, and then kill it with a solid plan, grit, and determination.

Get a Grip on Your Own Growth

In 1989, a Philadelphia financial analyst bought an old painting that displayed a depiction of a country scene. He'd purchased it for four dollars at a flea market in Adamstown, Pennsylvania because he was attracted to the framework of the painting. The buyer noticed a tear in the canvas, and the frame fell apart in his hands while trying to detach it from the painting. It was then that he discovered a folded document that appeared to be an old copy of a historically rare piece of Americana: The Declaration of Independence.

It was stored between the canvas and the wood backing. Interestingly enough, it was only after a friend who collected Civil War memorabilia advised him to have it appraised that he learned that the document was, in fact, a rare Dunlap broadside. One of five hundred official copies of the first printings of the Declaration of Independence from 1776!

This great document was offered for sale by Sotheby's in 1991 and brought in a sum of 2.42 million dollars! It was one of twenty-four known copies of the Declaration, and only one of three remaining in private hands at the time.

A Sotheby's spokesperson later told MSN News that the same Declaration of Independence copy was auctioned again in 2000 for a whopping 8.14 million dollars to movie producer Norman Lear and Internet entrepreneur David Hayden.

This is not a legend; it's a true story that began with four dollars at a flea market with a man that, ironically, wasn't attracted to the painting itself, but simply to its frame. Only to discover that there was a fortune at the flea market within the frame. There was something so much more valuable within this piece than what was initially perceived. What appeared to be in an average place, with a mediocre appearance, turned out to be something great. How many of you want to go to the flea market and get a find like this one? People are going to start ripping open old canvases to see if there's greatness lying beneath the surface of what they see.

I wonder if you truly know your marriage's value. Do you know your essential worth and significant importance? There's great potential that lies within your home. At first glance people may think they've got you figured out, but do they know that there's something of great value within the framework of what they see?

When we speak of a *great family legacy,* we define great as considerably above average, or of outstanding significance and importance. What I'm hoping you'll discover in your marriage is that it's time to tear open your framework. Get past the outward appearance of your canvas. Peak beyond your perceived limitations and discover the **greatness** within you. You are strategically placed in this world to live considerably above average. To build a great family, one of outstanding significance and importance.

Consider this, had there not been a tear in the canvas, he never would've dug deeper to discover what was beneath the surface. Something may be breaking within your heart. You may be in the middle of a life crisis or a pivotal moment where you need answers. Maybe the earthquake within your home was designed to break through the mundane, unveiling the magnificent. The greatness within you is crying out for introspection.

If you are sick and tired of living in an average and mediocre marriage, know that within you, there are dreams and visions that need to come to fruition. There's talent and potential underneath that hasn't fully been utilized, dreams that haven't been actualized, and something's got to change. You both need to lead on another level.

I remember in school, they taught us the difference between the adjectives good, better, and best. They also taught us the difference between bad, worse, and worst. I'd like to say that that painting was at its worst, while it was collecting dust at the flea market. It didn't belong there, and it was so undervalued. It was good when the discovery of what was within was uncovered, but when it was authenticated and confirmed as an original, it became as it was originally, great.

You may be at your worst right now in life. Maybe you believe that you're doing "good". Either way, I'd encourage you to continue to dig deep within to discover your true value and greatness. After all, as Jim Collins says, "Good is the enemy of great."

While everyone else is determined to waste time, how about investing in yourself? On average, we breathe about twelve to fifteen breaths per minute and seventeen thousand breaths per day. That's six million breaths taken per year! What are you doing to develop yourself with the breaths you consume? Hopefully, you're determined to make every second count towards leaving a great legacy.

How badly do you want to build wealth and get out of debt? Do you value gaining and maintaining a healthy lifestyle? Is it absolutely vital that you start a business that'll impact the world and change your family line? I pose to you this question, what's holding your home back from becoming great?

We believe God may allow trouble to provoke a transformation in you. This season is designed to bring some things that need to change to the surface. He's not focused on fixing your circumstance; His goal is to challenge the leader within you. Changing the quality of your character, so you'll be enabled to bear the quantity of His blessing. If you don't like where you are, discover what God desires to transform in you. Becoming a better parent, spouse, son, or daughter is contingent on your connection to God's power and participation in His plan. Getting a grip on your growth means you realize the need to develop on a daily basis intentional actions that influence your family in positive ways. You're not loosely living life wishing for better. Why? Because you realize that a great legacy is on the line! You've got no time to waste. A great story has been written by God, himself, with plans to prosper you, to give you a hope and a future. But you've got to play your part in the life-narrative that lies before you.

Looking back at moments where I struggled to lead, I find traces of fear. In trying to avoid repeat failures, I gave up on trying new things. Thinking that "safe" was better than being sorry again. But as Craig Groeschel once said, "The pathway to your greatest potential is straight through your greatest fears. Not taking risks ultimately leads to failure." This, I know to be true. While nestled in my bubble of risk-free behavior, I didn't realize I was volunatarily opting-out of my own growth. I became the failures I'd made and wore mistakes as a mask overlaying my identity. But I know now that I am not what I did; I am who God says I am!

CONCLUSION

AS YOU FACE UNFORESEEN SITUATIONS, BE IT GOLDEN OPPOR-
tunities, or a family crisis, when the time comes to respond, be sure
to make your decision together. Choose unity rather than unilateral
choices. Take on transitional problems as a team because a divided
house cannot stand. Under the pressures of life, the family literally
implodes from the very individuals who build it. But where there is
unity, the home is instantly strengthened. Ephesians 4:3 says, "Make
every effort to keep yourselves united in the Spirit, binding yourselves together with peace." The idea here is that we must strive.
Striving means to put in the work to preserve unity through peace.
Let there be a ceasefire against your spouse and an all-out assault
against every attack against your marriage.

There are real forces diligently fighting to divide your marriage &
destroy your family. But when you proactively combine your energy
to fight as a unified team, you'll win. Live fully awake to the war for
your relationship. Satan knows he must divide your unity to conquer
your family. Dr. Tony Evans made a powerful statement that altered
our perspective forever. He said, "Whoever owns the family, owns the
future." Worldviews are gravitating further and further away from
Biblical values. Refuse to allow unhealthy societal norms to erode
the integrity of your home. Contend for your territory. Undeterred by
uncertain times. Submit your willpower to God's power. Refusing to
allow any form of double-mindedness amidst the conflicts that arise.
Your legacy is on the line! And with so much at stake, you cannot
stop. Sean and I truly believe that whoever wants the family most will
have it. So instead of allowing transitions to rip you apart, guard your
hearts. Don't let Satan's divisive seeds of bitterness, unforgiveness,

or confusion germinate during those seasons. Work together with a tenaciousness towards unity. No matter what, put up a fight for your family's future.

While it's true that some change is unpredictable, over time, you instinctively begin to look ahead for oncoming critical decisions. For instance, you can clearly see your parents are aging and may need a plan for care, teenagers are on their way to college, or physiological changes as your bodies age. Navigating "foreseen" events is much easier when you make a habit of walking out the wisdom that we've shared in this book. The stronger your teamwork during predictable times, the greater the trust in the unpredictable seasons. So, when unforeseen circumstances take place, you will have normalized effective communication as a way of life. This empowers you to control the things you can while working through all of the unpredictable craziness you can't.

If you've found yourself overwhelmed by a transition, don't drown when you're surrounded by an ocean of support. Reach out and attain professional help. With the utmost respect for local pastors, close friends, and family members, they aren't professional counselors or therapists. There's nothing wrong with reaching out to your pastor for spiritual guidance, but after you've done that, please seek out a trauma therapist to help you reconcile big trauma or little trauma. Research bible-based marriage counselors, or even sex therapist if that's what's needed. Maybe you've tried one and didn't have a compelling experience. Don't quit! Keep going until you find the right fit. That doesn't mean settle for the person who only tells you what you want to hear. Sometimes great counsel challenges you, uproots unhealthy things, and stretches you to new levels. Think of it like this, if your car breaks down, you don't quit driving altogether. You head to the car dealership and search through the myriad of options until you purchase a more reliable vehicle. Don't wait till it's too late to connect with your mentors, small group leaders, or friends for sharpening your skills. Know that you are not alone. Throughout our years of pastoring people, we've encountered amazing people who gave themselves to everyone else. Pouring their lives into others whenever they were in trouble. But when they're in need, they don't want to "inconvenience" or "bother anyone." This mindset couldn't be further from the truth. You're not someone's problem. Those you consider family, people you know support you, are willing to help you through your time of need.

Now that you've read *Marriage in Transition*, the question emerges, what will you do with it? You're aware of the arsenal aboard your ship while navigating life transitions, so use them with discipline and rigorous commitment. When answering the questions posed in these pages, your life begins to come together. And you'll gain a sense of tranquility as you gain traction.

However, should you choose to passively engage in the fight for your family, you might very well forfeit the amazing legacy God entrusts you to steward. By now, you understand, it's not just what you know, but what you do with what you know now that counts. The truth is, your marriage is either getting better, or it's getting worse. There is no neutral ground. Passive couples tend to float wherever the current pushes their boat. Over time, they end up in a place far from their heart's desire, but those who want their marriage the most, will do what they must to have a successful marriage.

At our lowest moment as a couple, we contemplated divorce. As tensions mounted and efforts to communicate broke down, we consistently kicked around the idea of calling it quits. We were living in a world of offense and eventually saw one another as the enemy. Yet despite all of that, we truly loved one another. We just didn't have the wisdom to steer the ship in the right direction. One day, our lives changed when we decided divorce was not an option. We arrived at a point where we said, "We will do whatever it takes to fight for family. We're in this for the long haul." Twenty-two years in, and we can testify, it was the best decision to stay the course. And as you apply these concepts, you, too, can secure your family legacy.

May God's influence flow within and throughout every aspect of your life. Our prayer is for your family to manifest Psalm 112. That every husband and wife will prosper and lead well in a marriage of excellence. That people will recognize the blessing on your family. And finally, you rewrite your family line and walk in the promises of God.

ACKNOWLEDGEMENTS

OUR LIVES HAVE BEEN INFLUENCED BY SO MANY PEOPLE. There's no doubt that the greatest impact that has shaped our lives for the better are our children. Thank you, Brandon, Brianna, and Brittani. You support us in everything we do, and it's because of your sacrifice that we were able to follow our dreams. We pray this book allows you to enlarge your territory beyond where we've ever gone. Thank you for being on this journey with us. S.L.B-3 for Life!

There are so many nuggets of gold evident in our lives, and many of them stem from our life mentors, Kevin and Sonjia Dickerson. Thank you for sharing your wisdom, liberally, and with genuine love. Throughout our sixteen-year relationship, you were always there when we needed guidance and embraced us as family. It has been such a privilege to witness you generously pour your lives into so many families, and we are grateful to call you our spiritual Mom and Dad.

To our Pastors, Aaron and Lauren Kennedy, none of this would have happened without your support. First off, we're grateful for your friendship. The two of you truly model the Kingdom of God, and your passion for the sanctity of marriage and family is admirable. Thank you for believing in us and for giving us the privilege of serving with you at Opendoor Church.

ABOUT SEAN AND LANETTE REED

FOR 12 YEARS, THE REEDS HAVE SPOKEN TO THOUSANDS OF people at marriage conferences, workshops, retreats, and churches. Speaking at the XO Marriage Conference, the largest marriage conference in the world, as well as the Lakewood Church Marriage Retreat in Houston, TX. Traveling regularly throughout the country on a mission to build families that leave legacies.

Sean is a published author of two books, *Not Just Roommates: The Roadmap to Marriage Intimacy* and *God of the Valley: How to Navigate Through the Valleys of Life While Maintaining Hope.*

Sean & Lanette have over 250,000 views on their YouTube videos that provide marriage coaching for couples. The Reeds live with their three kids in Greenville, NC, where they're the Marriage and Family Pastors of Opendoor Church.

Follow the Reeds on social media:
Facebook: /seanandlanette
Instagram: @seanandlanette
YouTube channel: Life with Sean and Lanette